Following Directions

Recipe
1. _____
2. _____
3. _____

Following Directions

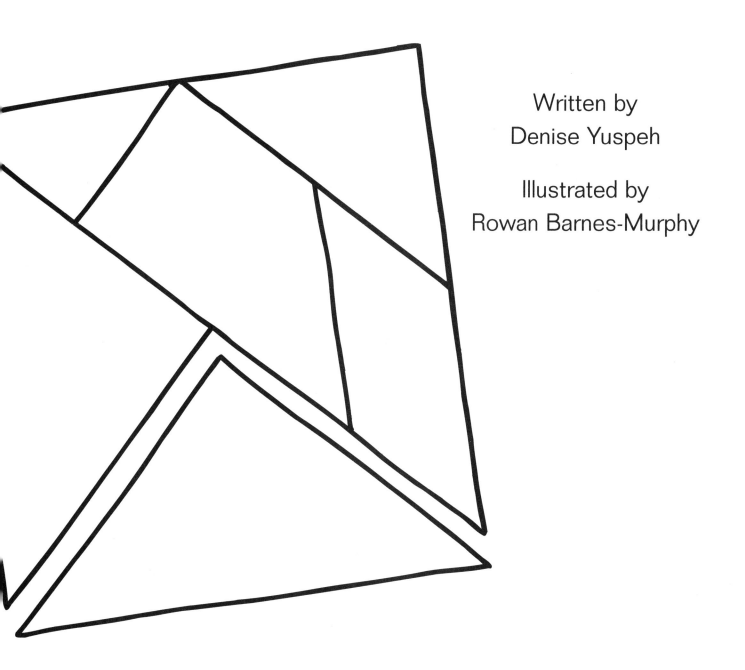

Written by
Denise Yuspeh

Illustrated by
Rowan Barnes-Murphy

Newbridge Educational Publishing

The purchase of this book entitles the buyer to duplicate these pages for use by students in the buyer's classroom. All other permissions must be obtained from the publisher.

Published in 1999 by Newbridge Educational Publishing, 333 East 38th Street, New York, NY 10016. © 1984 by Macmillan Educational Company. All rights reserved.

ISBN: 1-56784-714-5

10 9 8 7 6 5 4 3 2

Dear Teacher,

Among the most valuable skills you can teach your students are those related to giving and following directions. The FOLLOWING DIRECTIONS book is specially designed to help you give your students the opportunity to develop these skills, so important for success in and out of school.

The first section of this book, Math and Maps, allows your students to explore various types of maps and sharpen their thinking and organizational skills. They will "Shape Up!" their map skills, working individually or with partners to solve "Mystery Map" and other fun problems. By discovering the answer to "Where Is It?" your class can practice graphing skills while learning the importance of following directions in the order given. As students enter "The Land of Glee" and "Hometown," they better understand the value of a wide variety of maps. Finally, they will get "All Shook Up!" as they follow the directions for making a mathematical milk shake.

In the Reading and Writing section, students catch up with the "Signs of the Times" and develop the observational skills basic to following directions correctly and successfully. Your class will learn "How to Go from Here to There" in an exercise that helps strengthen and hone writing skills. The practicality of following directions step-by-step is stressed as students learn how to make "Daffy Taffy" and carefully read the ingredients in "Bingo's Biscuits."

The Projects and Games section contains creative activities such as "Kite Time" and "Helicopter," in which students carefully read and analyze the steps that will help them to complete their art projects. In "Let's Play I" and "Let's Play II," your students heighten listening skills through games involving giving directions to and taking them from other students. "Carrot Patch" provides fun and challenging ways to practice thinking and planning ahead.

The Mind-Benders and Mazes section helps prepare your class to unravel the logic and discrimination problems that they will encounter in many testing situations. Students work to learn how to join a "Secret Club" and how to identify each identical quadruplet in "Crazy Quads." Have your class figure out the secret message sent down by the "Flying Saucers" and discover the unusual path in "All Roads Lead to Rome." "Puzzling Plots" is a brainteaser that will help develop clear thinking as your students solve some baffling problems. "Categories" is an exciting game requiring nimble minds as students expand their facility with words.

In the last section of this book, Tests and Forms, your students deal with money problems in "Toy Store Math" and help sell bubble gum in "Bubble Boom!" "Make a Choice" provides practice in taking multiple-choice tests, and "True or False?" asks just that. In "Summer Camp," your students are introduced to the logistics of application forms, and "Space Helmet" explains the importance of filling out a warranty.

The FOLLOWING DIRECTIONS book provides many hours of challenging activities while it reinforces your students' abilities to think logically and give and follow directions in all subject areas.

Sincerely,

Anne Buckingham
Editor

Following Directions

CONTENTS

	Page	Grade Level	Reading Skills	Writing Skills	Math Skills	Language Skills	Thinking Skills	Science	Social Studies	Arts & Crafts
Section 1—Math and Maps										
A-maze-ing Math	7	2–3			•		•			
Mystery Picture	8	3	•		•		•			•
All Shook Up!	9	3–4	•		•					
Just Visiting	10	3–4	•		•		•			
Picture the Park	11	3–4	•				•		•	
Hometown	12	3–4	•				•		•	
The Land of Glee	13	3–4	•		•		•		•	
Shape Up!	14	3–5	•	•		•	•			
Go with the Flow	15	4–5	•		•		•			
Where Is It?	16	4–5			•		•			
Feline Express	17–18	4–5	•		•		•			
Mystery Map	19–20	4–5	•		•		•		•	
Time Out	21	4–5	•		•		•		•	
Awards	22									
Answers	23									
Section 2—Reading and Writing										
Mystery Words	24	2–3	•			•	•			•
Is It Real?	25	2–3	•				•			•
Maze-a-rama Town	26	2–4	•				•		•	
Road Signs	27–28	2–5	•			•	•			
Fairyland Crossroads	29	3–4	•				•		•	
Signs of the Times	30–31	3–4	•				•			
Bingo's Biscuits	32–33	3–4	•	•	•	•	•			
Daffy Taffy	34–35	3–5	•		•		•			
Line Up for the Parade	36	3–5	•				•			
Rhyme Time	37	3–5	•	•		•	•			
How to Go from Here to There	38	3–5	•	•			•			
One, Two, Three, Go!	39	3–5	•				•			
Dinosaur Days	40	4–5	•			•	•	•		
Animal Daze	41–42	4–5	•				•			
Answers	43–44									
Section 3—Projects and Games										
Shadow Play	45–47	2–3	•				•			•
Puzzle Picture	48–49	2–3	•				•			•
Carrot Patch	50–52	2–4	•		•		•			
Picture Charades	53–54	2–4				•	•			
Boomerang	55	2–4	•				•			•
Let's Play I	56	2–4				•	•			
Let's Play II	57	2–5				•	•			
Kite Time	58–59	2–5	•				•			•
Money Magic	60	2–5	•				•			
Wiggly Jigsaw Puzzle	61	2–5	•				•			•
Other Jigsaw Puzzle Ideas	62	3–5	•				•			•
Puzzle Cubes	63–66	3–5	•				•			•
Helicopter	67–68	4–5	•				•			•
Award	69									

Following Directions

CONTENTS

	Page	Grade Level	Reading Skills	Writing Skills	Math Skills	Language Skills	Thinking Skills	Science	Social Studies	Arts & Crafts
Section 4—Mind-Benders and Mazes										
Nutty Maze	70	2–4	•				•			
Fearful Flibbertigibbets	71	2–4	•				•			
Trace-a-Path	72	2–4	•			•	•			
Dots and Squares	73–74	2–5	•				•			
Secret Club	75	3–4	•				•			
Crazy Quads	76	3–4	•				•			
Flying Saucers	77	3–4	•				•			
Fruity Tree	78	3–4	•			•	•			
All Roads Lead to Rome	79	3–4	•				•			
Tangram Teasers	80	3–4	•				•			•
Tangram Dot-to-Dot	81	3–4	•				•			•
Categories	82	3–5	•	•			•			
Mrs. Periwinkle's Puppies	83	4–5	•				•			
Puzzling Plots	84	4–5	•				•			
Just Desserts	85	4–5	•				•			
Answers	86									
Section 5—Tests and Forms										
Paddling Along	87	2–3	•			•	•		•	
Animal Sillies	88	2–3	•			•	•			
Toy Store Math	89	3–4	•		•		•			
Match Them Up	90	3–4	•		•		•			
Class Questionnaire	91–92	3–5	•	•	•		•			
Summer Camp	93	3–5	•	•		•				
Bubble Boom!	94–95	4–5	•	•	•		•			
Space Helmet	96	4–5	•	•			•			
Make a Choice	97	4–5	•			•	•			
True or False?	98	4–5	•			•	•	•		
As Mr. Crowe Flies	99–100	4–5	•		•		•			
Teddy's Bear	101–102	4–5	•	•			•		•	
Outer Space News	103	4–5	•	•			•			
Awards	104–105									
Answers	106									

Name _____

A-MAZE-ING MATH

Blub, blub! You're stuck in a bubble maze! The only way to get out is to make a path through the magic bubbles. Not all the bubbles are magic—the magic ones all have problems that result in the number 7. Write 7 in the correct boxes, and trace your path out of the maze. When you are finished, color in the magic bubbles.

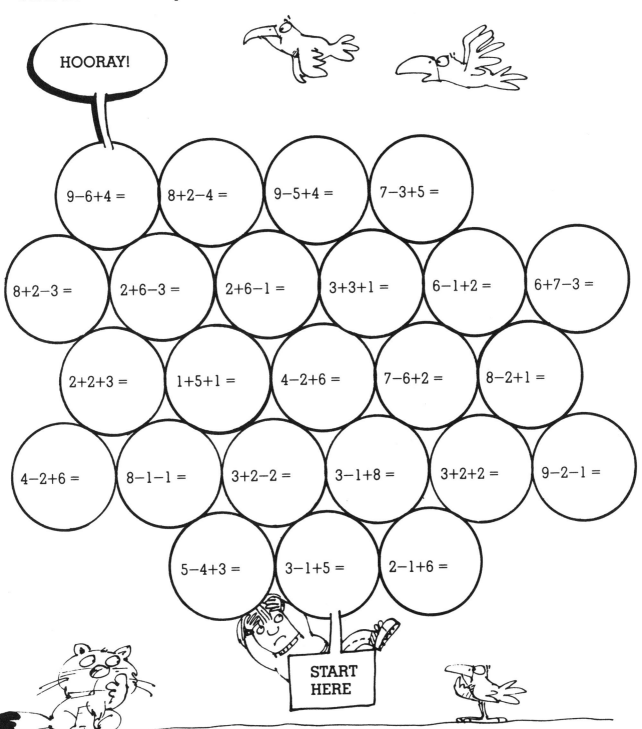

Name _____

MYSTERY PICTURE

Follow the directions below to find out what the mystery picture is.

1. Solve the math problems in each space.
   On the lines provided, write your answers.

2. Color red all the spaces with the answer 8.

3. Color orange all the spaces with the answer 9.

4. Color yellow all the spaces with the answer 6.

5. Color green all the spaces with the answer 7.

6. Color blue all the spaces with the answer 5.

7. Color violet all the spaces with the answer 3.

8. Leave white all the spaces with the answer 10.

9. Color brown all the spaces with the answer 4.

10. What is the mystery picture? _____

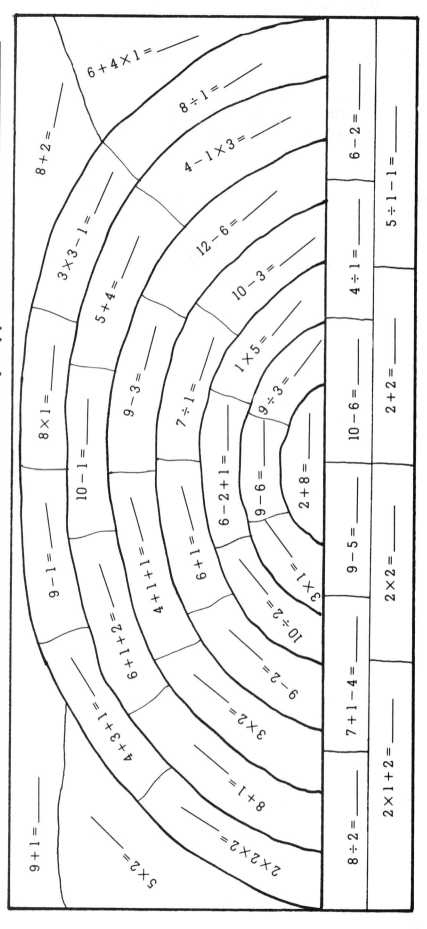

Name _____

ALL SHOOK UP!

Uh-oh! The big blender mixed up all the directions for Spunky's math milkshake. Using a separate sheet of paper, follow the directions in order from 1 to 20. If you do this carefully and correctly, you will find out how many scoops of ice cream Spunky needs to use.

12. Divide by 9 _____

6. Divide by 3 _____

16. Divide by 2 _____

11. Multiply by 2 _____

18. Subtract 17 _____

2. Divide by 4 _____

15. Subtract 1 _____

7. Add 40 _____

5. Add 4 _____

1. Add 6 and 6 _____

10. Add 12 _____

19. Add 10 _____

13. Subtract 2 _____

17. Multiply by 3 _____

3. Multiply by 6 _____

9. Subtract 3 _____

4. Subtract 7 _____

14. Add 15 _____

8. Divide by 5 _____

20. Subtract 9 _____

9

Name _____

JUST VISITING

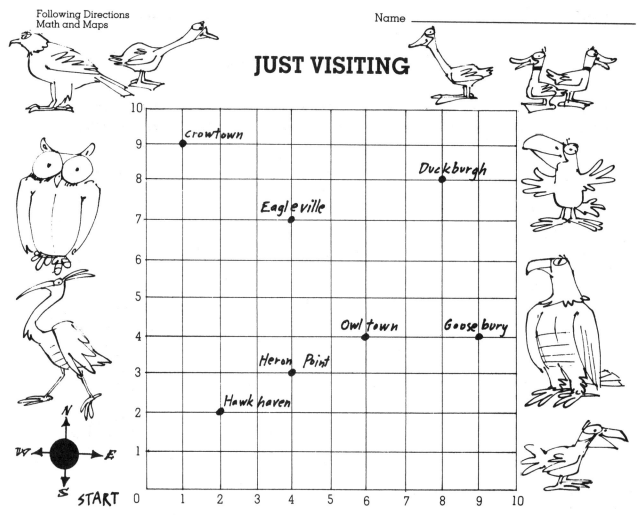

Gary and Grace Goose want to visit five towns, but they need your help.
Below are the directions to the five towns. To find each town, begin
at START. Next, use the directions and compass to guide you on the graph.
Then, in the spaces provided below, give the coordinate pair and the name of
each town. (Remember: The first number of the coordinate pair must tell how
many spaces to the right the town is. The second number must tell how many
spaces up the town is.)

Go east 6. Go north 4. Go west 3. Go west 1. Go south 2.	Go east 2. Go north 8. Go south 5. Go north 1. Go east 7.	Go north 3. Go north 6. Go east 7. Go west 4. Go west 2.	Go east 1. Go north 5. Go east 3. Go north 3. Go east 4.	Go north 9. Go south 4. Go east 6. Go west 2. Go north 2.
1. At what co- ordinates do they arrive? (,) What town is there? _____	2. At what co- ordinates do they arrive? (,) What town is there? _____	3. At what co- ordinates do they arrive? (,) What town is there? _____	4. At what co- ordinates do they arrive? (,) What town is there? _____	5. At what co- ordinates do they arrive? (,) What town is there? _____

Name _____

PICTURE THE PARK

Look at the picture of the park below. Complete sentences 1-5, using the directions north, south, east, and west. Then follow the instructions in 6-10 to finish drawing the picture of the park. The first answer has been done for you.

1. The entrance is on the _____east_____ side of the park.

2. The exit is on the _____ side of the park.

3. The lake is on the _____ side of the park.

4. The trees are on the _____ side of the lake.

5. The playground is on the _____ side of the park.

6. Draw two children on the east side of the park.

7. Draw one tree on the east side of the lake, and one tree on the west side of the lake.

8. Draw a dog on the road north of the lake.

9. Draw a child south of the playground.

10. Draw a duck on the north shore of the lake.

Name _____

HOMETOWN

This is a map of Sarah's hometown. She knows where everything is. Do you? Look at the map to help you answer the questions below. On the lines provided, write your answers.

park		Sarah's house	alley	Jan's house		library
	Street	Lee's house		Carla's house	Street	
		Ed's house		Tony's house		

Grand Avenue

| movie theater | shoe store | Oak | bank | grocery store | Pine | school |

1. On which street is Sarah's house? _____

2. How many houses are on Sarah's street? _____

3. What is behind the houses? _____

4. What street and avenue are next to the park? _____

5. Tony's house is on the corner of Pine Street and _____ Avenue.

6. What store is next to the movie theater? _____

7. Do you have to cross a street to go from the grocery store to the bank? _____

8. How many houses are on Pine Street? _____

9. How many streets does Sarah have to cross to get to the park from school? _____

10. Is the school closer to Sarah's house or to Ed's house? _____

Name _____

THE LAND OF GLEE

The Happy Harrigans are going on their vacation to the Land of Glee. Look carefully at the map of the Land of Glee below. The numbers along each piece of the road show the distance between one intersection and the next. Referring to the map and the key, answer the questions below. (Be sure to take the **shortest routes**.)

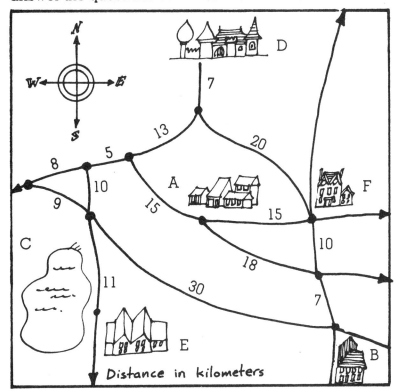

KEY

A — Shoppers' Village
B — High-Spirits Hotel
C — Lovely Lake
D — Perfect Palace
E — Ho-ho Hotel
F — Happy Hotel

Distance in kilometers

1. What is the nearest hotel to the Perfect Palace? _____

2. How far is the route from that hotel to the Perfect Palace? _____

3. What is the nearest hotel to Lovely Lake? _____

4. How far is the route from that hotel to the Perfect Palace? _____

5. If you started at the Ho-ho Hotel, went to visit friends at the High-Spirits Hotel, and finally went to the Happy Hotel for dinner, how far would you have traveled altogether? _____

6. How long is the shortest route from the Perfect Palace to the Shoppers' Village?

_____

7. Which hotel is farthest west? _____

8. Which has a shorter route to the Perfect Palace—the Ho-ho Hotel or the High-Spirits Hotel? _____

9. What is the distance of this route? _____

10. How long is the next-shortest route from this hotel to the Perfect Palace? _____

Name _____

SHAPE UP!

sample geometric shapes:	circle ○ triangle △ square □ rectangle ▭ parallelogram ▱ hexagon ⬡ pentagon ⬠ octagon ⯃ semi-circle ◓
sample designs:	

Materials: paper   **Optional:** ruler
pencil

Procedure:

1. Work with a partner. You will each need your own copy of this page. On a separate sheet of paper, each of you should draw a design using only simple geometric shapes (see examples of shapes and possible designs above).

2. Then, on the lines provided below, write down directions for drawing your design.

3. Trade directions with your partner, but don't show each other your designs. See if you can re-create each other's designs just by following the written directions.

4. Compare your friend's design to your original design. How close are they? Discuss how you might change the directions to make them clearer or easier to follow.

5. Give this page to your partner to write his or her evaluation of your directions.

Directions written by _____

1. _____
2. _____
3. _____
4. _____
5. _____
6. _____
7. _____
8. _____
9. _____
10. _____

Evaluation written by _____

_____

_____

_____

Name _____

GO WITH THE FLOW

Flowcharts are used for giving directions in a specific, logical order. Different types of directions are written in different-shaped boxes.

Look at the flowchart below. It shows you how to make a *palindrome*. A palindrome is a number (or word) that reads the same backward and forward. Look at the example.

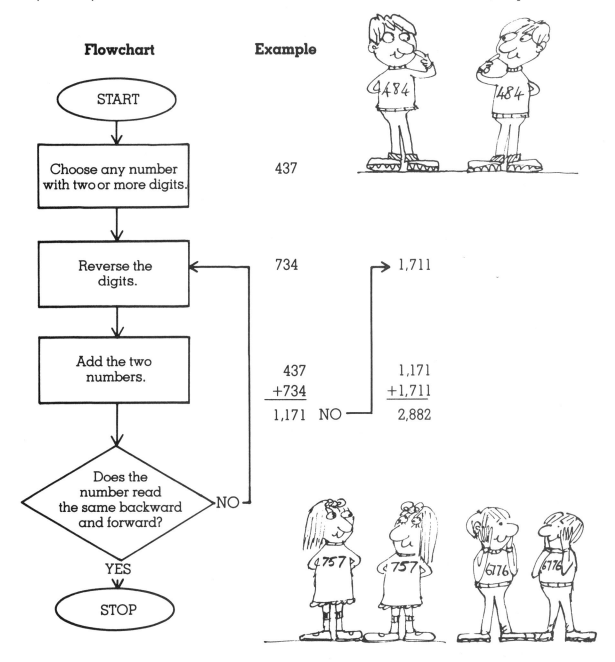

Flowchart

START

Choose any number with two or more digits.

Reverse the digits.

Add the two numbers.

Does the number read the same backward and forward?

NO

YES

STOP

Example

437

734   1,711

```
 437      1,171
+734     +1,711
1,171 NO  2,882
```

Use the flowchart above to find palindromes for the numbers below. You may need to take several steps with some problems to find the palindromes. Use a separate sheet of paper to show your work.

1. 29   2. 75   3. 95   4. 186   5. 238

Name _____

WHERE IS IT?

Louisa has lost something very important. To help her find it, follow these instructions. First look at the example of coordinate pair (2, 4) on the right. The first number of the pair tells you how many spaces to move to the right. The second number tells you how many spaces to move up. Plot the coordinate pairs below on the graph. Then connect all the points, using the directions in the box on the right below. The first point has been drawn for you.

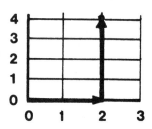

Coordinate Pairs

(2,4)	(3,6)
(4,6)	(5,7)
(6,8)	(7,9)
(8,12)	(12,13)
(13,10)	(9,8)
(1,1)	(1,2)
(3,4)	(2,3)
(5,6)	(4,5)
(7,8)	(6,7)
(10,13)	(8,9)
(12,8)	(13,12)
	(2,1)

Connect the Points

(1,1) to (1,2)	(7,8) to (7,9)
(1,2) to (2,3)	(7,9) to (8,9)
(2,3) to (2,4)	(8,9) to (8,12)
(2,4) to (3,4)	(8,12) to (10,13)
(3,4) to (3,6)	(10,13) to (12,13)
(3,6) to (4,5)	(12,13) to (13,12)
(4,5) to (4,6)	(13,12) to (13,10)
(4,6) to (5,6)	(13,10) to (12,8)
(5,6) to (5,7)	(12,8) to (9,8)
(5,7) to (6,7)	(9,8) to (2,1)
(6,7) to (6,8)	(2,1) to (1,1)
(6,8) to (7,8)	

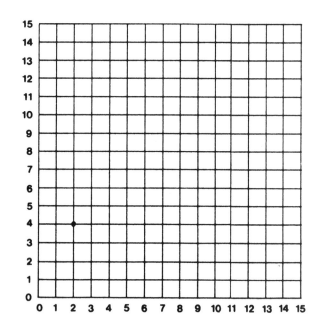

FELINE EXPRESS

In Alleycatville, everyone travels by Feline Express. Below is a map of Alleycatville, with the fares and schedule information for the Feline Express. Look at this page carefully, and use the information on it to answer the questions on page 18.

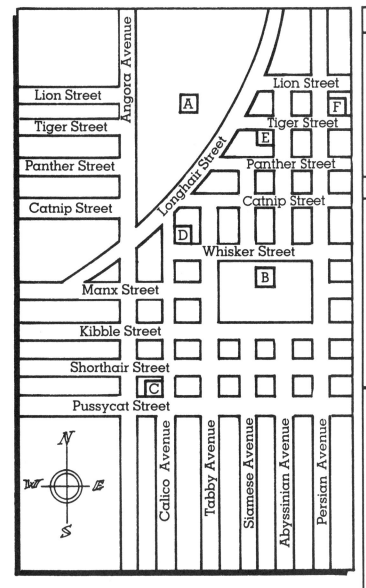

Fares to all stops	
Adults	90¢
Senior citizens (over 62 years old)	45¢
Students	45¢
Children (under 5 years old)	free

Feline Express schedule

Effective May 1st

Feline Express Bus Lines
27 Panther Street
Alleycatville, CT 09090
(191) 442-8442

★ ★ ★ ★ ★

Buses run every ½ hour from 7:00 A.M. to 11:00 P.M., following the schedule shown.

Schedule for 7:00 A.M bus:

	Stops	Times
1	Pussycat Street (at Persian Avenue)	7:00
2	Calico Avenue (at Pussycat Street)	7:15
3	Longhair Street (at Calico Avenue)	7:30
4	Panther Street (at Longhair Street)	7:35
5	Tiger Street (at Persian Avenue)	7:45
6	Persian Avenue (at Manx Street)	8:00

Location Key

A	Park	D	School
B	Shopping Center	E	Library
C	Museum	F	Movie Theater

Name _____

FELINE EXPRESS

Refer to page 17 to answer the questions below.

1. How many minutes does it take the Feline Express to go from stop 1 to stop 2? _____
_____

2. If the 7:00 bus leaves stop 1 five minutes late, what time will it reach stop 5? _____
_____

3. How long does it take to reach the stop near the school from stop 1 on the Feline
Express? _____

4. What is the name and number of the Feline Express stop nearest the museum? _____
_____

5. What's the name of the Feline Express stop nearest the movie theater? _____
_____

6. What are the numbers of the two Feline Express stops near the library? _____
and _____

7. Along which street or avenue does the Feline Express run between stops 1 and 2?
_____

8. How many blocks east and how many blocks north of the school is the library? ____
_____

9. Jamie, age 11, is a student at the Catland school. She and her grandfather, age 75,
are riding the Feline Express. How much is their fare together? _____

10. Mrs. Mill is going to the shopping center with her two-year-old child on the Feline
Express. How much is their fare together? _____

Name _____

MYSTERY MAP

Maps not only show direction—north, east, south, and west—but they also show distances. Usually a map has a *scale*, which tells you the distance from one place to another. Look at the scale below. The scale of this map is 1 centimeter (cm) for every 10 kilometers (km), so two places that are 1 cm apart on the map are actually 10 km apart.

The legend shows symbols for different features on the map. Draw in the symbols on the map by using the scale below and the directions on page 20. Once you've completed the map of the island, answer the questions at the bottom of page 20.

SCALE: 1 cm = 10 km

LEGEND

1. 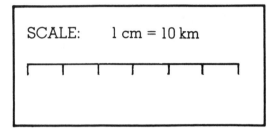 = campground

2. = lake

3. = mountains

4. = airport

5. = town

6. = forest

7. = boating dock

8. = river

9. ========= = road

10. = castle

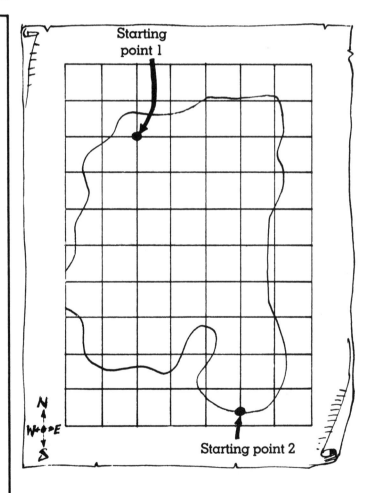

Starting point 1

Starting point 2

N
W←→E
S

MYSTERY MAP
Directions and Questions

Directions:

1. Go 10 kilometers (km) south and 20 km east of starting point 1. Draw symbol 1 there.

2. Go 10 km south and 10 km east from starting point 1. Draw symbol 2 there.

3. Go 30 km south from starting point 1. Draw symbol 3 there.

4. Go 40 km south and 10 km west from starting point 1. Draw symbol 4 there.

5. Go 40 km south and 10 km east from starting point 1. Draw symbol 5 there.

6. Go 25 km north from starting point 2. Draw symbol 6 there.

7. Go 70 km north and 15 km east from starting point 2. Draw symbol 7 there.

8. Go 10 km east and 5 km north from starting point 1. Mark a point. Then go 10 km south from this point. Mark another point. Draw symbol 8 between these two points.

9. Draw symbol 9 between symbol 4 and symbol 5.

10. Go 10 km north and 5 km west from starting point 2. Draw symbol 10 there.

Questions:

1. Which direction is the lake from the town? _____

2. To get to the airport from the town, in which direction must you go?

   _____

3. Which direction is the lake from the river? _____

4. Which direction is the boating dock from the lake? _____

5. How many km is it from the town to the airport? _____

6. How many km is it from the town to the lake? _____

7. How many km is the campground from the lake? _____

8. How many km south and west must you go to get to the castle from the forest?

   _____ south and _____ west

9. How many km south and west are the mountains from the campground?

   _____ south and _____ west

10. How many km north and east must you go to get to the campground from the town?

    _____ north and _____ east

Name _____

TIME OUT

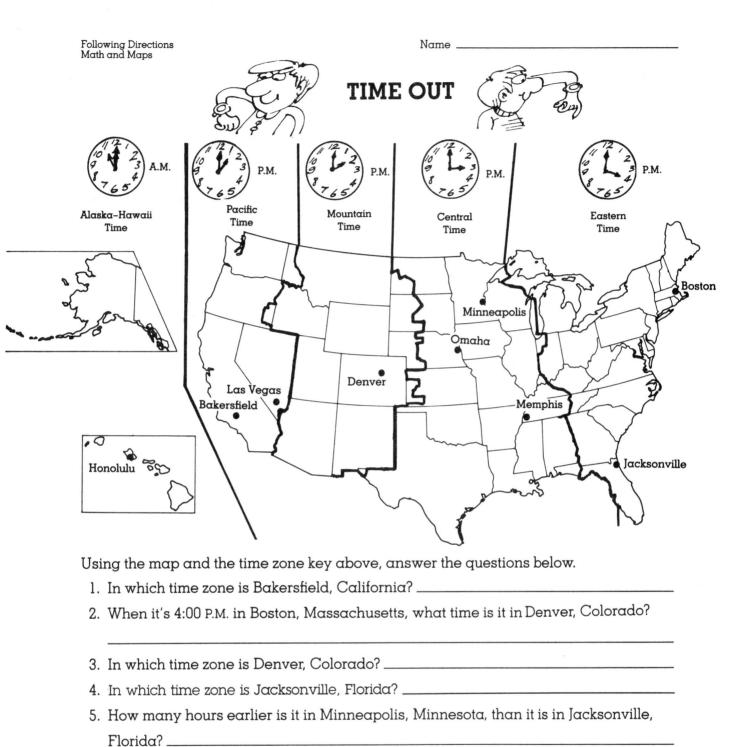

Alaska–Hawaii Time   Pacific Time   Mountain Time   Central Time   Eastern Time

Using the map and the time zone key above, answer the questions below.

1. In which time zone is Bakersfield, California? _____

2. When it's 4:00 P.M. in Boston, Massachusetts, what time is it in Denver, Colorado?

   _____

3. In which time zone is Denver, Colorado? _____

4. In which time zone is Jacksonville, Florida? _____

5. How many hours earlier is it in Minneapolis, Minnesota, than it is in Jacksonville,

   Florida? _____

6. How many hours later is it in Omaha, Nebraska, than it is in Denver, Colorado?

   _____

7. In which time zone is Las Vegas, Nevada? _____

8. In which time zone is Memphis, Tennessee? _____

9. When it's 4:00 P.M. in Boston, Massachusetts, what time is it in Las Vegas, Nevada?

   _____

10. When it's 3:00 A.M. Monday in Jacksonville, Florida, what day and time is it in

    Honolulu, Hawaii? _____

AWARDS

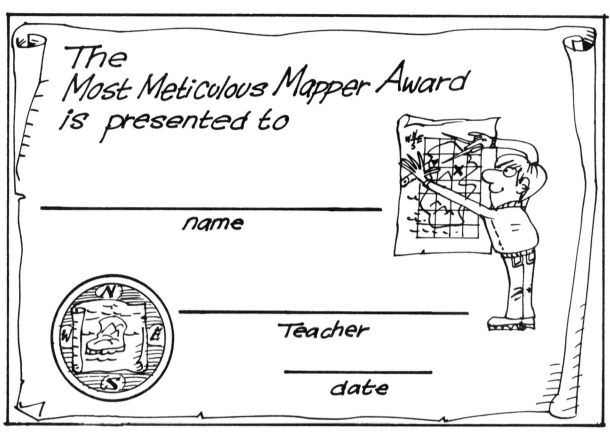

The
Most Meticulous Mapper Award
is presented to

_____
name

_____
Teacher

_____
date

The Magical Mathematician Award
is presented to

_____
name

_____
Teacher

_____
date

Answer Sheet for *Math and Maps*—Section 1

A-maze-ing Math—page 7

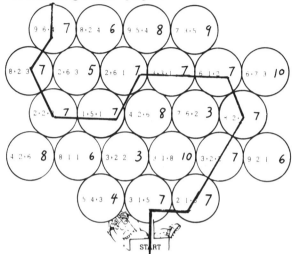

Mystery Picture—page 8

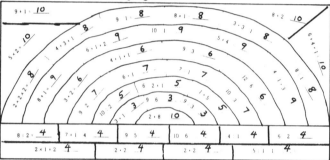

10. a rainbow

All Shook Up!—page 9

eight scoops of ice cream

Just Visiting—page 10

1. (2, 2) Hawkhaven
2. (9, 4) Goosebury
3. (1, 9) Crowtown
4. (8, 8) Duckburgh
5. (4, 7) Eagleville

Picture the Park—page 11

2. south
3. north
4. south
5. west

6.–10. Drawings will vary. Check to see that each figure is placed correctly.

Hometown—page 12

1. Oak Street
2. three
3. an alley
4. Grand Avenue and Oak Street
5. Grand
6. shoe store
7. No.
8. three
9. three
10. Ed's house

The Land of Glee—page 13

1. Happy Hotel
2. 27 km
3. Ho-ho Hotel
4. 46 km
5. 58 km
6. 35 km
7. Ho-ho Hotel
8. High-Spirits Hotel
9. 44 km
10. 60 km

Go with the Flow—page 15

1. 121   2. 363   3. 1,111   4. 6,996   5. 1,771

Where Is It?—page 16

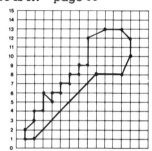

Feline Express—page 18

1. 15 minutes
2. 7:50 A.M.
3. 30 minutes (or ½ hour)
4. Calico Avenue (at Pussycat), stop 2
5. Tiger Street (at Persian)
6. Stops 4 and 5
7. Pussycat Street
8. three blocks east and three blocks north
9. 90¢
10. 90¢

Mystery Map—page 20

1. north
2. west
3. south
4. east
5. 20 km
6. 30 km
7. 10 km
8. 15 km south and 5 km west
9. 20 km south and 20 km west
10. 30 km north and 10 km east

Time Out—page 21

1. Pacific
2. 2:00 P.M.
3. Mountain
4. Eastern
5. one
6. one
7. Pacific
8. Central
9. 1:00 P.M.
10. 10:00 P.M. Sunday

Name _____

MYSTERY WORDS

Follow the directions to discover the mystery words.

1. Color the spaces with the animal words red.

2. Color the spaces with the food words blue.

3. Color the spaces with the clothing words purple.

4. Color the spaces with the furniture words green.

24

Name _____

IS IT REAL?

Some of the sentences below describe things that are true, and some describe things that are make-believe. Read each sentence below. If it describes something that is true, follow the directions to draw the picture using a pencil and crayons. If it tells you something make-believe, don't draw the picture. (Use a separate sheet of paper for drawing.)

1. If a horse can fly, draw a green circle.
2. If a dog has two eyes, draw an apple.
3. If you go to school, draw a flower.
4. If a pencil can talk, draw a blue square.
5. If frogs go to your school, draw a star.
6. If cars have wheels, draw two red triangles.
7. If a clock can walk, draw a blue circle and a blue triangle.
8. If a cat and a mouse are animals, draw a candy bar.
9. If a penny and a banana are both coins, draw three rectangles.
10. If cake is food, draw a green square and a red circle.

Name _____

MAZE-A-RAMA TOWN

In Maze-a-rama Town, everyone gets lost all the time. But you have the directions that
will lead you through the town. Pretend you are in a car, driving through the streets.
Carefully follow the directions below, and trace your path through the town.

1. Enter the town. Drive until you see the Amazing Toy Store and then turn left. Turn
   right just before you come to the Grange Garage.

2. Keep going straight until you pass the Central School, and then make a right.

3. Follow the road past the Wacky Movie Theater until it forks into three roads. Take
   the center road.

4. Keep going until you reach the grocery store. Turn left and then make another quick
   left.

5. Follow the road out of the city.

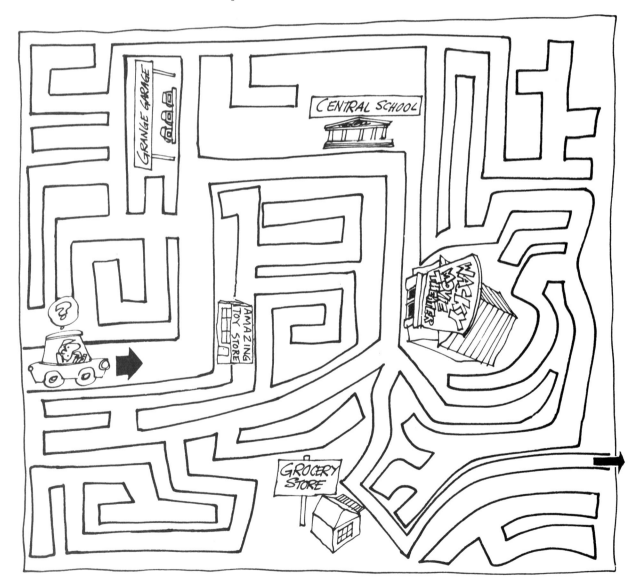

Name _____

ROAD SIGNS

Mandy and Randy Tandem are learning about road signs. These signs are used to give drivers and bicyclists directions and information. To the right of each sign below is its meaning. Study the signs and their meanings. Then look at the road signs on page 28.

 SCHOOL CROSSING

 CURVE AHEAD

 STOP

 WINDING ROAD

 YIELD

 SLIPPERY WHEN WET

 RAILROAD CROSSING

 NO RIGHT TURN

 ONE WAY

 NO LEFT TURN

ROAD SIGNS

After studying page 27, look at the page below. There are ten road signs in the two left columns. On the right are their meanings. Without looking at page 27, write the letter of the correct meaning on the line to the left of each road sign.

_____ 1.

_____ 6.

a. STOP

b. YIELD

_____ 2.

c. RAILROAD CROSSING

d. ONE WAY

e. NO RIGHT TURN

_____ 7.

f. NO LEFT TURN

_____ 3.

g. SLIPPERY WHEN WET

h. SCHOOL CROSSING

i. CURVE AHEAD

_____ 8.

j. WINDING ROAD

_____ 4.

_____ 9.

_____ 5.

_____ 10.

Name _____

FAIRYLAND CROSSROADS

The map of Fairyland below has several places to visit marked on it. The directions at the bottom of the page tell you how to get to each place. Look at the directions and match each one to the place it leads to. On each of the lines provided, write the letter of the correct place.

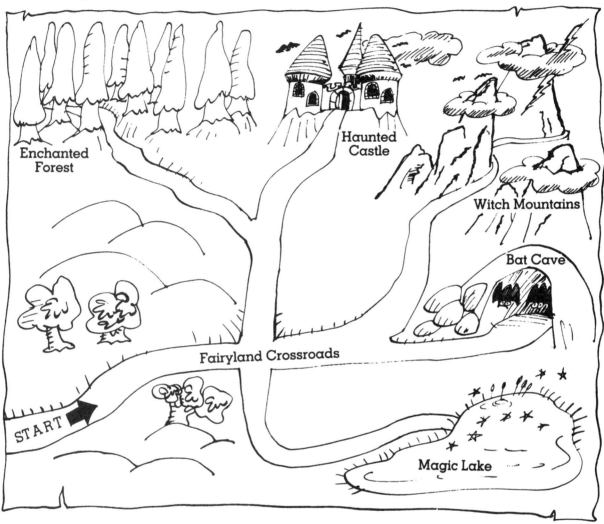

_____ 1. Go left at the crossroads and then left again at the next fork.

a. Haunted Castle

_____ 2. Go right at the crossroads and follow the road to the end.

b. Bat Cave

_____ 3. Go straight at the crossroads and keep going. When the road forks, bear right.

c. Magic Lake

_____ 4. Take the left-hand road at the crossroads, and when the road forks, take the right-hand road.

d. Witch Mountains

_____ 5. Go straight at the crossroads and keep going. When the road forks, keep left.

e. Enchanted Forest

Name _____

SIGNS OF THE TIMES

Here we are at the train station. It's filled with signs that give people directions or information. Look at the picture below very carefully. There are 20 signs altogether.

Then do the hidden-word wheel and the word-find puzzle on page 31. All of the words on the signs below appear in the two puzzles.

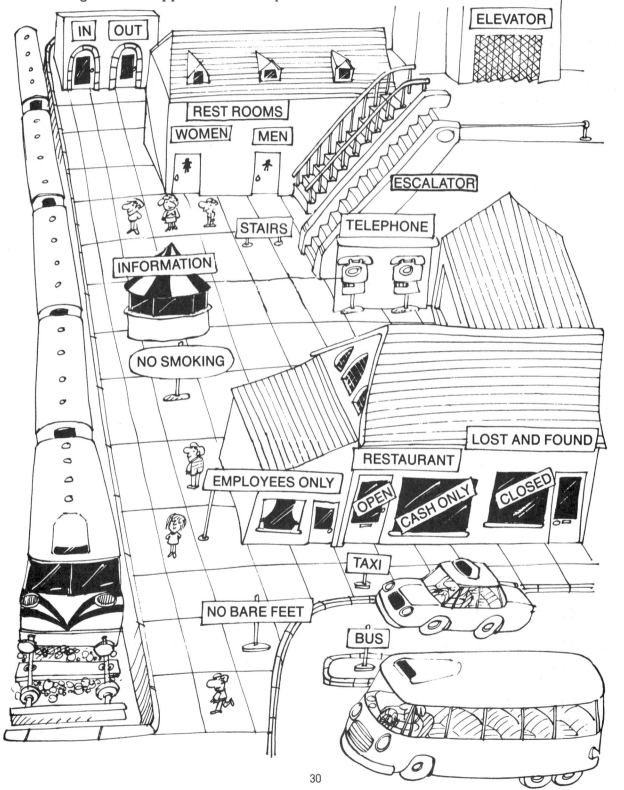

SIGNS OF THE TIMES

Look at the hidden-word wheel and the word-find puzzle below. The words on all 20 of the signs on page 30 are included in these two puzzles.

In the hidden-word wheel, draw a line to separate the words. The first one has been done for you.

In the word-find puzzle, search for and circle the hidden words. The words may be found horizontally, vertically, or diagonally. They may also be either forward or backward. The same letter may be used in more than one word.

Then check the words you found here with the words on the signs on page 30 to see if you found them all.

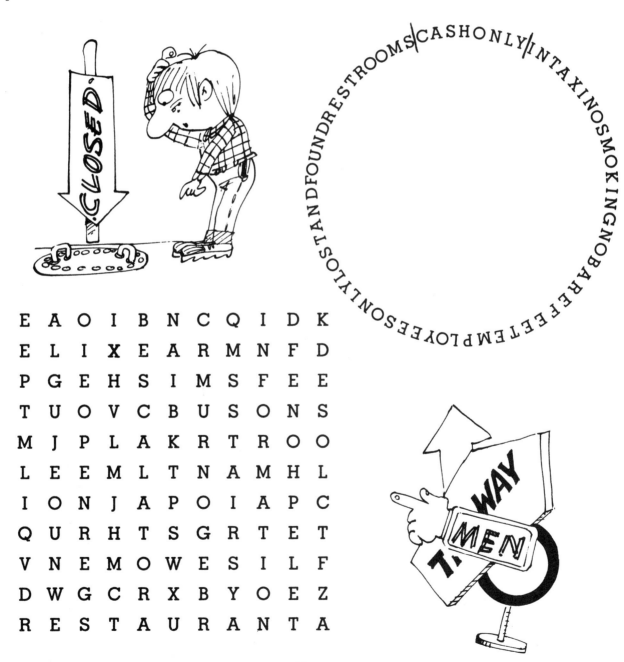

E A O I B N C Q I D K

E L I X E A R M N F D

P G E H S I M S F E E

T U O V C B U S O N S

M J P L A K R T R O O

L E E M L T N A M H L

I O N J A P O I A P C

Q U R H T S G R T E T

V N E M O W E S I L F

D W G C R X B Y O E Z

R E S T A U R A N T A

Name _____

BINGO'S BISCUITS

Bingo the dog is looking at his new box of Boffo Biscuits. Unfortunately, Bingo can't read the information and instructions on the box—but you can! Look at the box carefully and use the information on it to answer the questions on page 33.

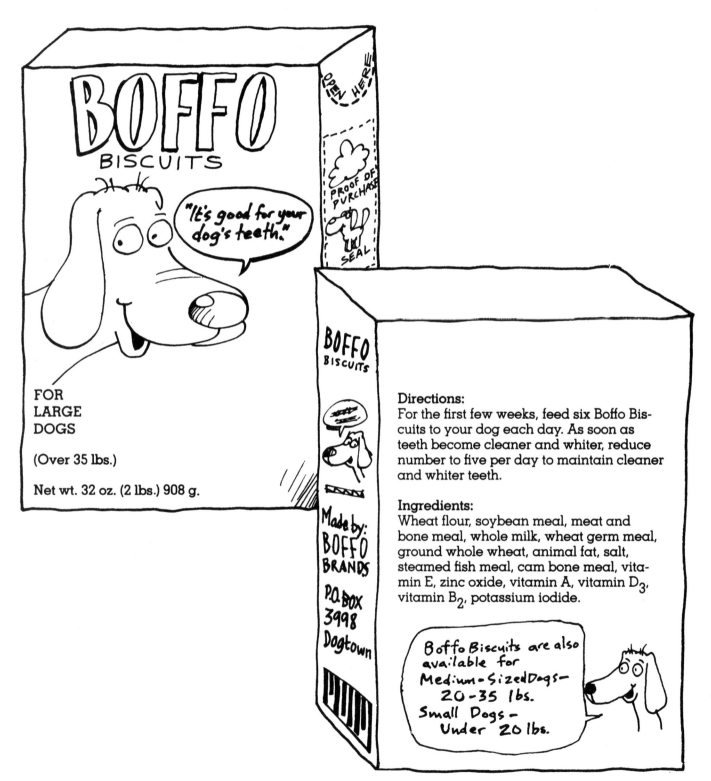

Name _____

BINGO'S BISCUITS

Using the information on page 32, answer the questions below.

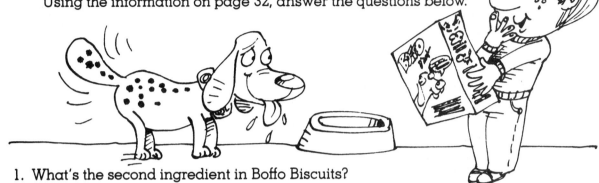

1. What's the second ingredient in Boffo Biscuits?

   _____

2. How many biscuits should you feed your dog each day for the first few weeks?

   _____

3. What size dog should eat the biscuits from this box?

   _____

There are three ways of describing how much this box of Boffo Biscuits weighs. List this weight in each of the units below, and use the correct abbreviations for each:

   4. ounces _____   5. pounds _____   6. grams _____

7. What is the Boffo Biscuits slogan? _____

8. Who makes Boffo Biscuits? _____

9. According to the directions, what will happen if you give your dog five biscuits per day?

   _____

10. If you need a Boffo Biscuits proof-of-purchase seal for a special offer, where would you find it on this box?

   _____

11. If you had a complaint or a question about Boffo Biscuits, where would you write?

   _____

List the last seven ingredients in Boffo Biscuits:

12. _____   13. _____   14. _____

15. _____   16. _____   17. _____

18. _____

19. What's the first verb in the directions? _____

20. What other size dogs are Boffo Biscuits available for? _____

Name _____

DAFFY TAFFY

It's Daffy Taffy Time! When making taffy (or anything else, for that matter!) it's a good idea to use a recipe. A recipe gives you a list of <u>what</u> you need to make the dish (the ingredients) and also instructions on <u>how</u> to make the dish (the directions). Look at the recipe for Daffy Taffy below, and use the information in it to answer the questions on page 35.

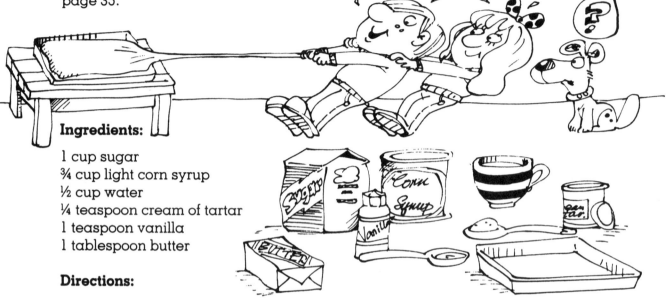

Ingredients:

1 cup sugar
¾ cup light corn syrup
½ cup water
¼ teaspoon cream of tartar
1 teaspoon vanilla
1 tablespoon butter

Directions:

1. Grease an 8″ × 8″ baking dish and put it aside until you're ready to use it.

2. In a saucepan combine the sugar, corn syrup, water, and cream of tartar.

3. Bring the mixture to a boil over medium heat and stir constantly until the sugar has melted (this will take about 10 minutes).

4. Continue to cook the mixture, without stirring, for about 30 more minutes. (If you have a candy thermometer, the mixture will be ready when the temperature reads 256° F. If you don't have a candy thermometer, you can test the mixture by dropping a small amount into a glass of very cold water. If it forms a hard ball, it's ready.)

5. Take the saucepan off the heat and stir in the vanilla and butter.

6. Pour the mixture into the greased dish and let it cool for 15 to 20 minutes. When the taffy is cool at the center (not just at the edges), then it's ready to be pulled.

7. Wash and dry your hands and rub some butter on them.

8. Take a handful of taffy and start pulling. If the taffy sticks, more butter on the hands will help. Keep pulling until the taffy has a satiny look to it and a milk-white color. (If the taffy becomes too hard to pull, heat it in a 350° F oven for a few minutes to soften it.)

9. Pull the taffy into long strips and cut it into pieces with scissors.

10. Wrap the taffy in plastic wrap.

Name _____

DAFFY TAFFY

Different Daffy Taffies:

• Try adding one tablespoon of your favorite flavoring (peppermint, chocolate extract, lemon extract) instead of the vanilla.

• Right after step 5, divide the mixture into two halves. Stir 8 to 10 drops of one food coloring into one half and the same amount of another food coloring into the second half. Then drop each mixture into its own greased dish. Follow steps 6 through 9 with each mixture, and then twist the differently colored pieces of taffy together.

Questions:

1. If you wanted to make twice as much taffy, how much sugar would you need altogether?
   a. 2 cups   b. 1½ cups   c. 3 cups   d. 1 cup

2. How many ingredients are there in this recipe?
   a. five   b. three   c. six   d. 1¾

3. How long do you let the taffy mixture cool before pulling it?
   a. 15 to 20 minutes   b. 10 minutes   c. 30 minutes   d. 10 to 15 minutes

4. What kind of cream does this recipe tell you to use?
   a. whipping cream   b. heavy cream   c. light cream   d. cream of tartar

5. What size baking dish does this recipe tell you to use?
   a. 8″ × 8″   b. 10″ × 12″   c. 15″ × 20″   d. 8″ x 10″

6. With what should you cut the taffy?
   a. a sharp knife   b. scissors   c. a saw   d. a butter knife

7. How may extra ideas are there for different daffy taffies?
   a. three   b. one   c. four   d. two

8. How hot should the mixture be after you cook it for about 30 minutes?
   a. 250° F   b. 256° C   c. 256° F   d. 350° F

9. About how long will it take for the sugar to melt while stirring the mixture constantly?
   a. 15 to 20 minutes   b. about 10 minutes   c. about 30 minutes   d. about 25 minutes

10. How much butter does this recipe say to use?
    a. 1 tablespoon   b. 1 teaspoon   c. 2 tablespoons   d. 1 cup

Name _____

LINE UP FOR THE PARADE

The circus parade is about to begin, and the performers need to line up. The sentences below tell how to put them in the correct order. Carefully read the sentences. Then, on each performer's sign, write the number of his or her place in line.

The clown will lead the parade.

The big bear will walk at the end of the parade.

The ringmaster will walk behind the clown.

The lion will walk behind the ringmaster.

The baby bear will walk in front of the big bear.

The horse will walk in front of the baby bear.

The dancing dog will walk behind the juggler.

The elephant will walk behind the lion.

The juggler will walk behind the elephant.

The bareback rider will walk in front of the horse.

RHYME TIME

Words rhyme when they have the same ending sounds. Some examples of rhyming words are *hair* and *care, rain* and *stain*. Many poems contain *couplets*. A couplet is two lines, one right after the other; each line ends with a rhyming word. Below is an example of a poem that contains two couplets.

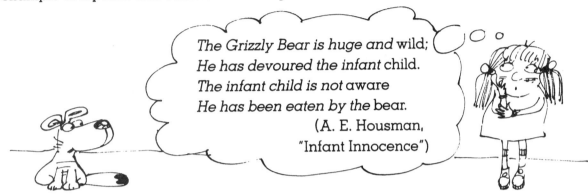

The Grizzly Bear is huge and wild;
He has devoured the infant child.
The infant child is not aware
He has been eaten by the bear.
(A. E. Housman,
"Infant Innocence")

Now write your own poem using couplets. Look at the list of rhyming words below. On another piece of paper, practice writing couplets that end with some of these rhyming words. Then, on the lines below, write a poem that contains couplets. Be sure to give your poem a title.

home	heat	see	right	trick	late	sing
roam	meet	me	light	stick	date	ring
gnome	feet	be	fight	quick	ate	bring
dome	eat	free	bite	lick	bait	sting

_____
title

_____

_____

_____

_____

_____

_____

_____

_____

_____

_____

Name _____

HOW TO GO FROM HERE TO THERE

Writing and following directions are very useful skills to have. Work with a friend to practice both skills in this exercise.

Each of you should have a copy of this page. Think of directions for traveling from one place to another in your classroom or your school. On the lines provided below, write down the directions. Exchange papers, leave your seats, and follow the written directions right up to the last step.

Directions written by _____

Traveling from _____

Traveling to _____

Directions: _____

_____

_____

_____

_____

_____

After following the directions, meet with your friend and evaluate each other's directions. On the lines provided on your friend's sheet, fill in your name and answer the questions.

Evaluation written by _____

Did you reach the right location? _____

Were the directions clear and correct? _____

Were any confusing or wrong? _____

How could they have been better? _____

_____

_____

_____

Name _____

ONE, TWO, THREE, GO!

See how quickly you can follow the directions below.

1. Read all the directions below before you do any of the activities.

2. Smile and blink your eyes twice.

3. Mark an **X** on all the triangles: △ △ □ △ ◇ ▽ □

4. Write the days of the week: _____

_____

5. Do these subtraction problems:
$$\begin{array}{ccccc} 8 & 6 & 7 & 9 & 10 \\ -2 & -4 & -3 & -1 & -5 \end{array}$$

6. Draw a picture of an apple.

7. Write your name here: _____

8. Write your teacher's name here: _____

9. Add these numbers together: $4 + 2 + 1 + 3 + 6 + 5 =$ _____

10. Write your favorite food: _____

11. Spell the word *dictionary* backward: _____

12. Write a word that rhymes with each of these words: mad _____   slow _____

eat _____   care_____

13. Write the name of your best friend: _____

14. Write the numbers from 1–10: _____

15. Now that you have read all of the directions beforehand, do only step 7.

Name _____

DINOSAUR DAYS

Read the article below. Then read the questions at the bottom of the page and write your answers in the correct spaces in the chart. (Hint: Not all of the spaces in the chart will be filled in.)

Dinosaurs ruled the earth before human beings existed. They ruled with great size and strength—the word *dinosaur* means "terrible lizard." Some dinosaurs were bigger than a house, and others were about the size of a chicken. Several dinosaurs walked upright on two legs and had two hands.

Dinosaurs had small brains, usually no larger than a walnut. That one tiny brain wasn't enough for them to control their huge bodies, so some of the larger dinosaurs had a second brain near their tails.

Scientists learn about dinosaurs by carefully studying fossils. By looking at fossil dinosaur teeth, you can tell if they ate meat or plants. Some things are harder to learn from fossils, and that makes dinosaur experts disagree. For example, were dinosaurs warm-blooded creatures (like people) or cold-blooded ones (like snakes)? This question and many others are still unanswered. We've only known about dinosaurs for about 150 years. New fossils are being discovered all the time. There's always more to learn about these "terrible lizards."

1. What is the first adjective in paragraph 1?

2. What are the first three nouns in paragraph 3?

3. What is the first verb used in this article?

4. What is the first adjective in the first sentence of paragraph 2?

5. What is the adverb in the last sentence of paragraph 1?

6. What is the first verb in paragraph 3?

7. What is the adjective in the second-to-last sentence of paragraph 3?

8. What is the adverb in the first sentence of paragraph 3?

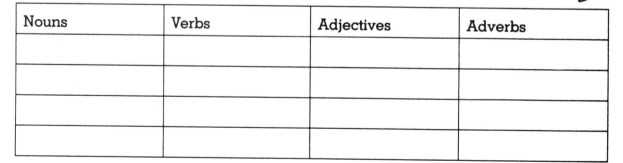

Nouns	Verbs	Adjectives	Adverbs

Name _____

ANIMAL DAZE

Use the directions on page 42 to help you complete the drawing below.

Name _____

ANIMAL DAZE

Follow the directions below to complete the drawing on page 41.

1. Divide the frame into four equal boxes.

2. In the upper left-hand box, write the number 1 in the upper left-hand corner.

3. In the upper right-hand box, write the number 2 in the upper left-hand corner.

4. In the lower left-hand box, write the number 3 in the upper left-hand corner.

5. In the lower right-hand box, write the number 4 in the upper left-hand corner.

6. In box 1, draw a big mouth, full of teeth, on the lion's face.

7. In box 2, draw a big piece of Swiss cheese next to the mouse.

8. In box 3, draw a face on the dog.

9. In box 4, draw a long tail and two pointed ears on the cat.

10. Over the drawing of the lion in box 1, draw six vertical lines for the bars of a cage.

11. Draw a smile on the mouse in box 2.

12. Draw a T-shirt on the dog in box 3.

13. On the cat in box 4, draw a triangular nose and three whiskers on each side.

14. At the bottom of box 1, write the words *Beware of Lion*.

15. At the top of box 2, write the words *Happy Mouse*.

16. On the dog's T-shirt in box 3, write the words *Super Dog*.

17. Draw a cartoon thought-balloon above the cat in box 4.

18. Draw whiskers on the mouse's face in box 2.

19. Write the word *Purr* in the cat's thought-balloon in box 4.

20. Draw a barbell in Super Dog's hands in box 3.

Answer Sheet for *Reading and Writing*—Section 2

Mystery Words—page 24

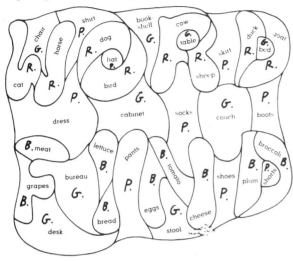

Is It Real?—page 25

Student should have drawn the following:
2. an apple
3. a flower
6. two red triangles
8. a candy bar
10. a green square and a red circle

Maze-a-rama Town—page 26

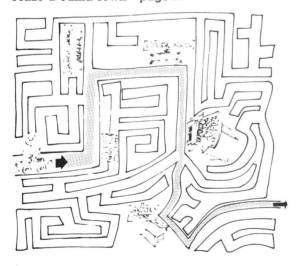

Road Signs—page 28

1. i   6. j
2. d   7. e
3. a   8. b
4. c   9. g
5. h   10. f

Fairyland Crossroads—page 29

1. e
2. c
3. b
4. a
5. d

Signs of the Times—page 31

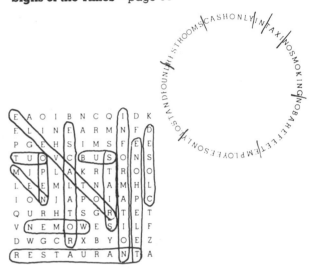

Bingo's Biscuits—page 33

1. soybean meal
2. six
3. a large one
4. 32 oz.
5. 2 lbs.
6. 908 g.
7. It's good for your dog's teeth.
8. Boffo Brands
9. The dog's teeth will stay cleaner and whiter.
10. on the side
11. P.O. Box 3998, Dogtown
12. cam bone meal
13. vitamin E
14. zinc oxide
15. vitamin A
16. vitamin D_3
17. vitamin B_2
18. potassium iodide
19. feed
20. medium and small

Daffy Taffy—page 35

1. a   6. b
2. c   7. d
3. a   8. c
4. d   9. b
5. a   10. a

Answer Sheet for *Reading and Writing*—Section 2

Line Up for the Parade—page 36

Rhyme Time—page 37

Student poems will vary, but should be checked for correct use of couplet rhyme scheme: aa, bb, and so on.

How to Go from Here to There—page 38

Answers will vary.

One, Two, Three, Go!—page 39

The page should contain only the student's name written in step 7.

Dinosaur Days—page 40

Nouns	Verbs	Adjectives	Adverbs
scientists	ruled	human	upright
dinosaurs	learn	small	carefully
fossils		new	

Animal Daze—page 41

SHADOW PLAY

Here are some ways you can have fun in a dark room, using shadows.

SHADOW PUPPETS

Materials: scissors
copy of the lion and mouse
   patterns on page 47
paste
two pieces of 9″ × 12″ cardboard
masking tape
two wooden sticks about 9″
   long
a flashlight

Procedure:

1. Cut out the copies of the lion and mouse patterns on page 47.

2. Paste each pattern onto a piece of cardboard and cut out the cardboard pattern.

3. With masking tape, attach a stick to the back of the pattern. (Instead, you may use several strips of 1″ × 9″ cardboard stacked atop one another and taped together.)

4. Turn out all the lights and turn on the flashlight.

5. Hold a shadow puppet in front of a blank wall and shine your flashlight on the puppet so that it creates a shadow on the wall.

6. Try moving your puppet closer to and farther away from the flashlight. Watch what happens to the shadow.

SHADOW PANTOMIME

Materials: white sheet
lamp
small sheets of paper, several for each student
pencil
box for papers

Procedure:

1. Hang a white sheet over a doorway and place a lamp four or five feet behind the sheet.

2. Seat the audience in front of the sheet.

3. Give each student a small piece of paper on which he or she must write an activity to be mimed. Mix the papers together in a box or a bag. Possible activities include eating dinner, hitting a baseball, jogging, swimming, or flying like a bird.

4. The mimic picks an activity and acts it out between the lamp and the sheet, while the audience tries to guess what he or she is doing. Everyone should get a chance to mime.

5. You can make your show more challenging by encouraging students to write activities that involve imitations of famous people or people familiar to your particular class.

6. You can also use costumes, old clothes, or props, which often cast interesting shadows.

SHADOW PLAY

SHADOW PUPPETS SHOW

You can use your shadow puppets to present the fable of "The Lion and the Mouse." Pick someone to read the story below, while two other students act out the story with the shadow puppets.

THE LION AND THE MOUSE

Aesop's Fable

In the jungle long ago, there lived an enormous lion. One day while taking a nap, he was suddenly awakened when a little mouse scampered over his face. The lion quickly seized the mouse in his paw and was just about to eat him when the mouse squeaked, "Please let me go. If you do, I will always remember your kindness. Someday I will help you."

The lion laughed to think that this small creature could ever help him, but he let the mouse go free. Sure enough, the day came when the lion was in great danger. As he was walking through the jungle one day, he suddenly was caught by a hunter's net, and he couldn't escape. He roared in anger so that all the animals could hear. When the little mouse heard him, he ran up to the net at once and started nibbling it. He gnawed and gnawed until he made a hole large enough so that the lion could escape. "I told you I would remember your kindness and help you," said the mouse. "You see, even a little friend can be a good one."

46

SHADOW PLAY
Patterns

Reproduce and distribute this page.

Mouse Pattern

Lion Pattern

Name _____

PUZZLE PICTURE

Follow the directions below to assemble the puzzle picture.

Materials: scissors
circle picture on this page
paste
cardboard
crayons

Procedure:

Cut out the circle picture below, paste it onto cardboard, and cut it out again. Then cut it into pieces along the thick black lines. Put the pieces together so the picture makes sense. You can color in the puzzle any way you like. Follow the directions on page 49 to make your own puzzle picture.

Name _____

PUZZLE PICTURE
Pattern

Materials: crayons
circle pattern on this page
scissors

Procedure:

Make a colorful drawing in the circle. Draw it as if the dotted lines are not there.
Then cut out the pieces on the dotted lines. Mix up the pieces, give them to a friend,
and challenge him or her to put the puzzle together.

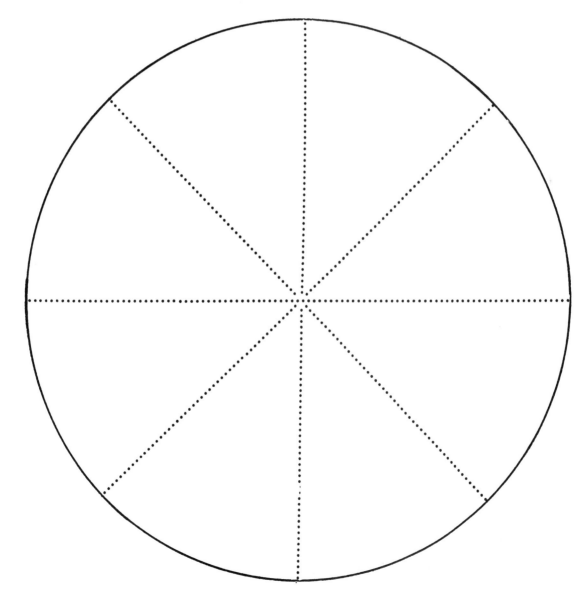

Name _____

CARROT PATCH

Carrot Patch is a game for two to four players. The object is to reach the end with the most carrots.

Paste a copy of the game board (page 52) on cardboard and cut out along dotted lines. Create the markers, cube, and carrots, by following the instructions on a copy of page 51.

 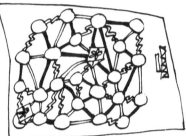 

Directions

1. Each player takes a carrot and a marker, and all markers are placed on START. Decide who will go first, second, and so on.

2. On your turn, throw the cube and look at the pattern on top when the cube lands. Go to the nearest carrot patch (a circle with a number) along the path that has the same pattern. For example, if the top of the cube is black, follow the black pathway, and so on.

3. When you get to the patch, take or give back as many carrots as it says. +1 means take one carrot from the envelope. −2 means give back two carrots. (You may move to a −1 patch only if you have one or more carrots. You may move to a −2 patch only if you have two or more carrots.) If you don't have any carrots left, you must stay where you are and wait for your next turn.

4. You can move in any direction (sometimes you may want to move backward so you can pick up more carrots).

5. The first player to reach the END of the Carrot Patch gets four more carrots. The game is over when all the players get to the END. The player with the most carrots is the winner!

Other Ways to Play the Game

• Play the game for five minutes only. When the time is up, whoever has the most carrots wins.

• Lightly pencil in 15 to 20 arrows along some of the patterned paths on the game board. These are now one-way paths. Play the game as above, except that you can't go backward on a one-way path. If a player can't move, he or she loses that turn. The game ends when the first player reaches the end.

• Cut out 20 squares of paper. All sides of each square should be ¾ inch. Play the game as directed, with this exception: after someone lands on a space (and picks or gives back the right number of carrots), cover that space with a piece of paper. Covered spaces may be landed on again and again. The game is over when the first player gets to the end.

Name _____

CARROT PATCH
Game Pieces

Carrots:

Cut out each carrot, and place all carrots in an envelope.

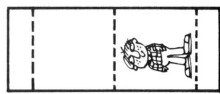

Cube and Markers

1. Cut out on the solid lines.

2. Fold the dotted lines to form figure.

3. Tape flaps under.

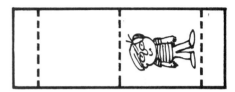

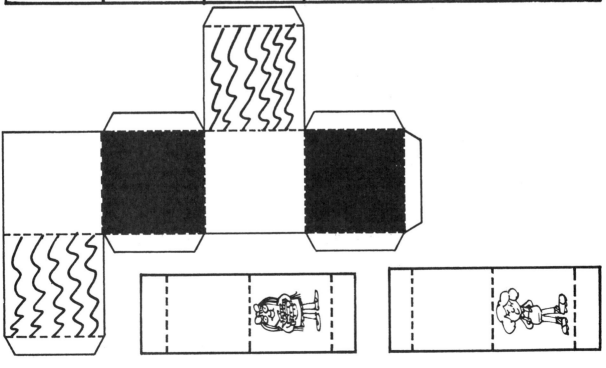

51

Name _____

CARROT PATCH
Game Board

Reproduce this page.

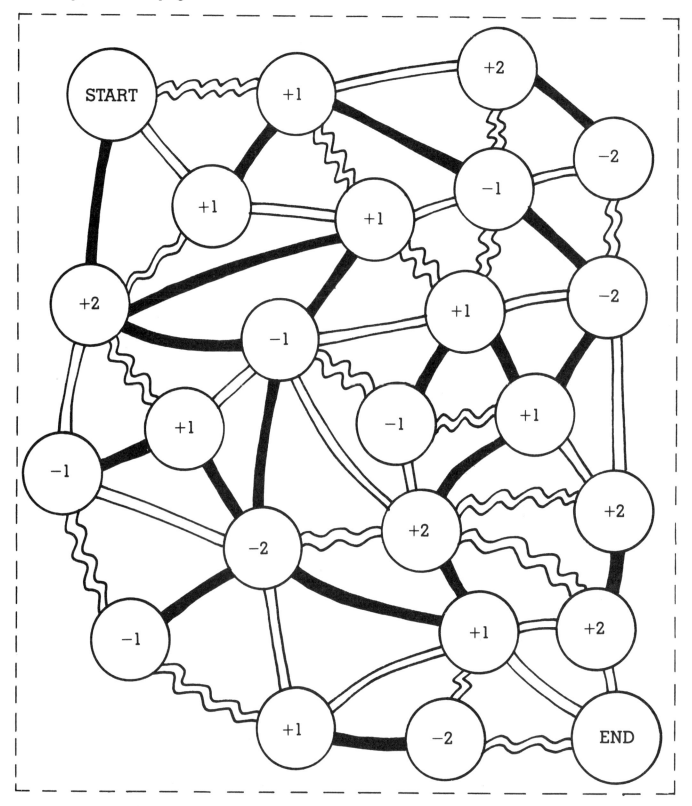

Name _____

PICTURE CHARADES

Here is a game you can play with one or more friends. To learn how to play, follow the directions below.

Materials: scissors
cards on this page and page 54

Procedure:

1. Cut out the cards on this page and on page 54.

2. Lay all the cards faceup on a table.

3. Choose one person to be "it." That person looks at all the cards and silently chooses one, without letting anyone know which one has been chosen.

4. Now, "it" acts out the picture on that card, while everyone else tries to guess which one it is. Whoever guesses correctly is "it" next time around.

For a harder version of this game, lay the cards facedown, or put them in a box or a hat, and have "it" choose one at random. Also, you can add to this game by making up your own cards.

TELEPHONE	BUMBLEBEE
AIRPLANE	HORSE
CLOCK	DOG

PICTURE CHARADES

Reproduce this page.

ELEPHANT

CAT

TRAIN

BIRD

CAR

RABBIT

ROBOT

GORILLA

SEAL

SANTA CLAUS

Name _____

BOOMERANG

Follow the directions below to make and fly a boomerang.

Materials: scissors
boomerang pattern on this page
pencil
9″ × 6″ pieces of cardboard or oaktag
crayons

Procedure:

1. Cut out the boomerang pattern on this page. Trace it onto cardboard or oaktag, and cut it out. Color it with crayons.

2. Stand in an open area. Hold your hand at eye level, about a foot from your face. Your palm should face downward.

3. Put the boomerang on the back of your hand. Make sure one wing sticks out over the edge of your thumb.

4. Hit the back edge of the wing with the index finger of your other hand. The boomerang should fly forward.

5. Keep practicing. You should soon be able to make the boomerang fly away and come back to you every time.

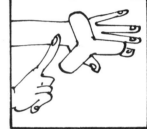

Another way to fly your boomerang:

1. Hold your hand at eye level, about a foot from your face. Your palm should face away from you. Hold the boomerang loosely between your thumb and index finger. It should be parallel to the floor.

2. Hit the back of one wing of the boomerang hard with the index finger of the other hand, as you let go of the boomerang.

3. Keep practicing till you can make it fly away and come back to you.

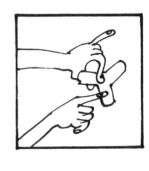

LET'S PLAY I

The following two games involve a group following directions given by a leader. Any number can play. After playing, it may be useful to discuss the importance of following rules and directions in different types of games and sports—and what happens if they are not followed.

Rules and Directions for Playing *Simon Says*

1. Stand in front of the group of players. Explain that everyone must do whatever you say—after you say the words "Simon says." For example: "Simon says, 'Hands on shoulders,'" or "Simon says, 'Touch your left ear with your right hand.'"

2. If you don't say "Simon says," players must ignore your instructions. Explain that any player who follows instructions not prefaced by "Simon says" is out.

3. Keep playing until only one player is left. That child can lead the next game. Let the children take turns leading the game.

Rules and Directions for Playing *Near and Far*

1. Explain that you will pick an object in the room, and you will give each player clues regarding whether he or she is near or far from the object. Determine the amount of time each player will have to find it.

2. Pick an object. Ask the first player to leave the room while you tell the rest of the class what the object is. When the child returns, ask him or her to walk around the room, trying to guess the object.

3. Give the child clues regarding his or her distance from the object. Clue words can be *near* and *far* or *hot* and *cold*. The pair of clue words you choose should be the only clues given. If the first player has not found the object within the time given, it is the next player's turn.

4. Keep playing until the object is located. The winner can then pick another object and lead the game.

LET'S PLAY II

The following two games involve a group listening to and remembering sequences of clues. Any number can play. After playing, it may be useful to discuss the importance of listening carefully and following the order in which things should be done. For example, do you sign a letter first and then write the message?

Rules and Directions for Playing *What Is It?*

1. Collect a large assortment of objects of different colors and shapes, and place them on your desk. The objects should have some attributes in common.

2. Explain that you will give clues describing one of the objects. The players must listen to and remember each clue, because you won't repeat any of them after you have given a new clue.

3. Give one clue for the object you have chosen. For example, if the object is a marble, your first clue might be that it is round.

4. Give the players each one chance to locate and name round things on your desk. If no one has guessed the marble, give a different clue. For example, you could say that it is mostly blue.

5. Keep giving clues until the object is identified. The winner can then choose another object and lead the game. An alternative to this is to let the winner collect an assortment of different objects and then lead the game.

Rules and Directions for Playing *Memory Words*

1. Explain that the object of this game is to add a word to a previously given word or phrase, making a longer phrase but not completing a sentence. If a person adds a word that completes the sentence, he or she is out.

2. On a sheet of paper, record the growing list of words so that the correct word order is kept during the game.

3. Determine the order in which the players take turns. The first player starts by saying one word. The second player repeats the first word and adds one. The next player repeats the first two words and adds a third. For example, the first player says, "Mister," the second player says, "Mister Jones," the third player says, "Mister Jones and." If the third player had said, "Mister Jones sings," he or she would be out, because that completes a sentence.

4. Play becomes more difficult as the phrases get longer. Each player gets two chances to repeat all the previous words in the right order. Play until only one person remains.

Name _____

KITE TIME

To make a kite, follow the directions below.

Materials:

paste
copy of the kite pattern on page 59
heavy construction paper
scissors
crayons, markers, colored pencils, or paints and a paintbrush
a 4″ by 24″ piece of tissue paper
stapler
clear tape
drinking straw
hole puncher
13″ piece of thread
ruler
spool of heavy thread or light string

Procedure:

1. Paste the kite pattern onto construction paper, and cut it out.

2. Paint or color all sides of the wings in whatever pattern or design you like.

3. Fold the kite down the middle line so that the wings meet at the top.

4. Cut the tissue paper into three strips for the tail, making sure the strips are connected on one end (see illustration).

5. Fold the tissue strips and staple to the back of the kite as shown.

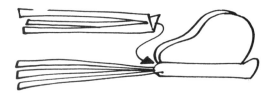

6. Fold the wings down as shown.

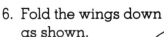

7. Tape the wings together on the TAPE HERE box.

8. Tape the straw to the wings on the TAPE STRAW HERE boxes.

9. Punch holes through the black dots in the front and the back of the kite and tie the 13″ piece of thread to the two holes.

10. Measure 2½″ on the thread, starting at the front end of the kite. Tie the end of the spool of thread here. You will fly your kite with this.

11. Go outside with your kite. Let out two feet of thread and run.

12. Let out more thread as the kite flies higher. Try to catch the wind!

Name _____

KITE TIME
Pattern

Follow the directions on page 58 to make this kite.

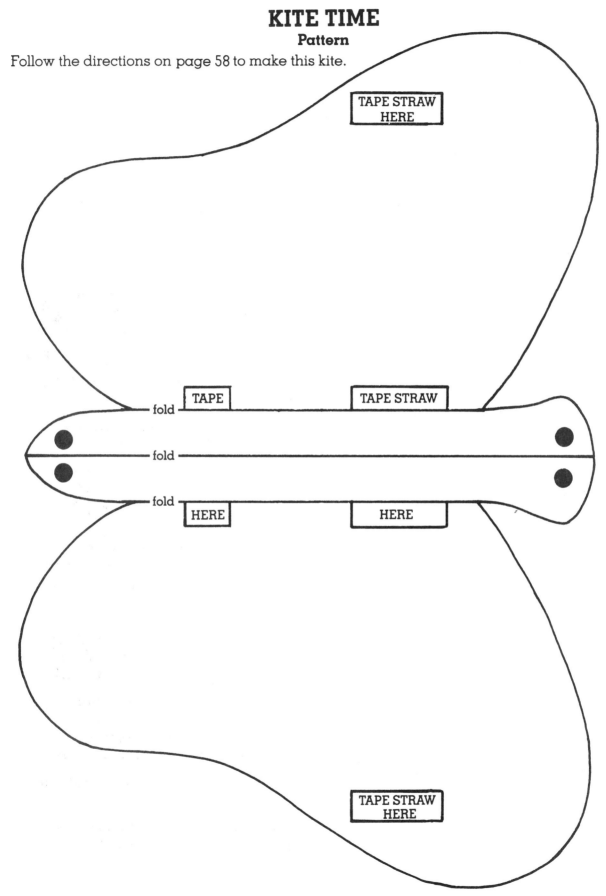

TAPE STRAW
HERE

fold — TAPE

TAPE STRAW

fold

fold — HERE

HERE

TAPE STRAW
HERE

Name _____

MONEY MAGIC

Here are three tricks you can do with play money. Just follow the directions below.

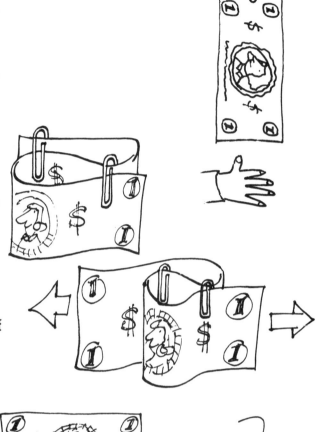

1. See how fast you and your friends are. Hold a play dollar bill by one end above a friend's hand. Let it drop and see if he or she can catch it sideways between his or her thumb and another finger. Now, let your friend drop the bill, and see if *you* can catch it.

2. Fold the bill in thirds, and attach two paper clips as shown.

   Quickly pull the ends of the bill away from each other (not <u>too</u> hard, or you'll tear it).

   Presto chang-o! The two paper clips are now clipped to each other!

3. Can you turn money upside down? Start with your play money right side up and facing you. Then fold the top of the bill toward you.

   Fold the bill toward you again.

   Now, fold the right side over the left.

   Unfold the back part of the fold out to the right.

   Unfold the first crease upward and away from you, as shown.

   Then open the bill—and it is upside down! Can you figure out how this trick is done?

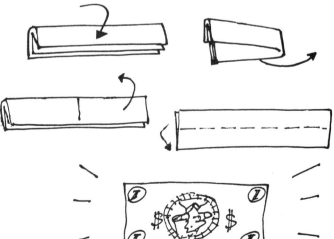

Name _____

WIGGLY JIGSAW PUZZLE

Here's a funny kind of jigsaw puzzle pattern. Color a picture in the rectangle below, ignoring the jagged lines. Then paste the rectangle onto cardboard and carefully cut out all the pieces. Mix the pieces up and put your picture back together. You can trade puzzles with a friend and see who can put a puzzle back together the fastest.

Name _____

OTHER JIGSAW PUZZLE IDEAS

Materials: crayons or markers
drawing paper
scissors
old magazine
paste
cardboard
pen or pencil

Procedure:

1. Make a large drawing, or cut out a picture from an old magazine. Paste the picture onto a piece of cardboard. Then take a pen or a pencil and draw jigsaw puzzle shapes on it. You may want to make the outline of the puzzle a special shape, like a circle, triangle, or square. If your puzzle is a drawing, you may even cut along the outline of the drawing. Make sure the pieces you draw are big enough for you to be able to cut them out. Then cut along the lines you have drawn. Mix up the pieces and put the puzzle back together.

2. Homemade jigsaw puzzles make great gifts. After you make a jigsaw puzzle, decorate a box with the same art you put on the jigsaw puzzle, mix up the pieces, and put them in the box.

Name _____

PUZZLE CUBES

Puzzle cube pictures are fun to solve. To make the four picture puzzles below, you **need** a set of complete puzzle cubes, made from the patterns on pages 64, 65, and 66.

First look at picture A. Use it as a guide while you put your puzzle cubes together to form the same picture. Then do the same with pictures B through F. After you are done, try putting the puzzles together without looking at the page.

A.

D.

B.

E.

C.

F.

Name _____

PUZZLE CUBES
Patterns

Cut out each cube on the solid lines.

Fold the cubes on the dotted lines.

Use clear plastic adhesive or glue to seal
the flaps.

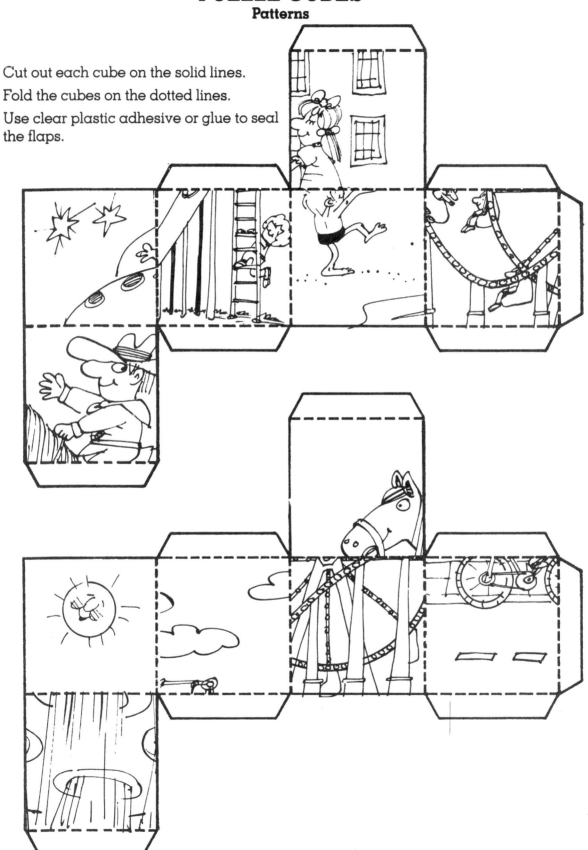

Name _____

PUZZLE CUBES
Patterns

Cut out each cube on the solid lines.

Fold the cubes on the dotted lines.

Use clear plastic adhesive or glue to seal the flaps.

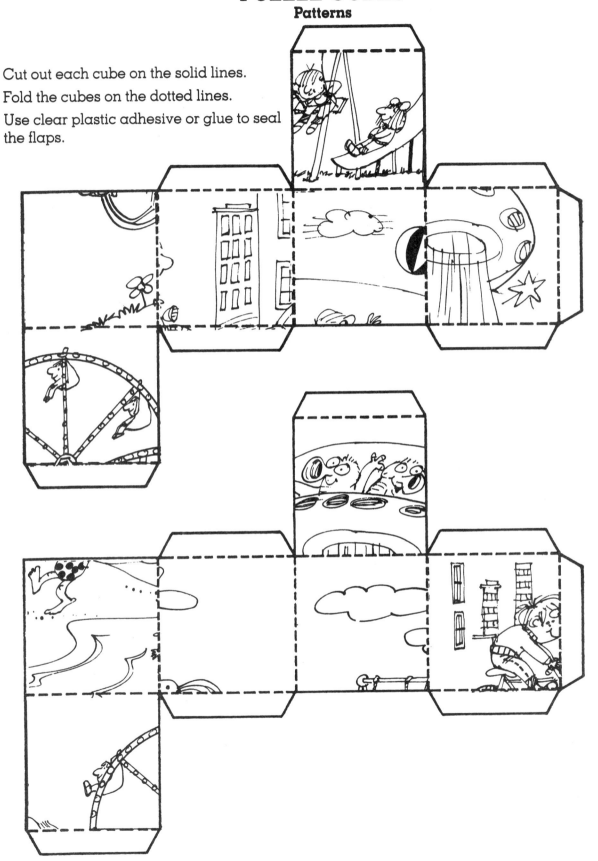

Name _____

PUZZLE CUBES
Patterns

Cut out each cube on the solid lines.

Fold the cubes on the dotted lines.

Use clear plastic adhesive or glue to seal the flaps.

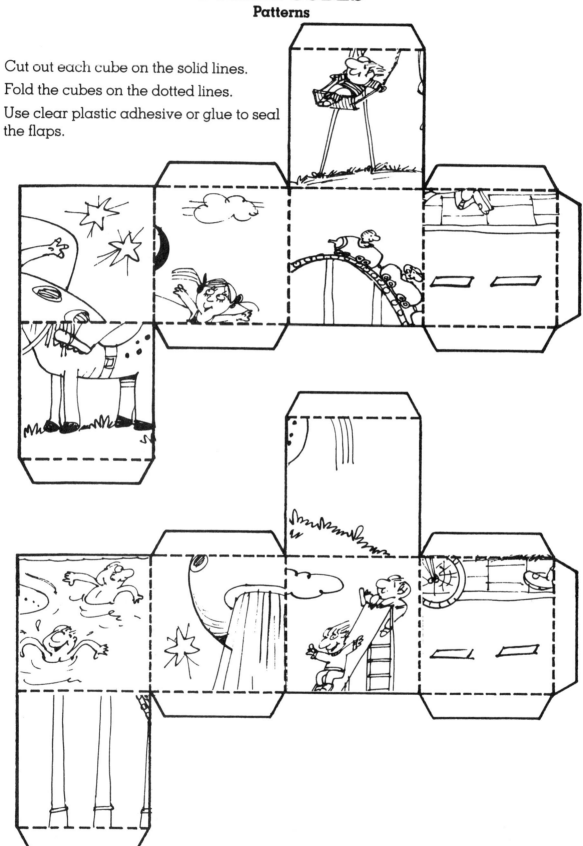

Name _____

HELICOPTER

Follow the directions below to make paper helicopters.

Materials: scissors
copy of helicopter patterns on page 68
pencil
9″ × 12″ construction paper
crayons
ruler
paper clip

Procedure:

1. Cut out the helicopter patterns on page 68. Trace them onto construction paper and cut them out. Color them with crayons.

2. Follow directions 3–6, using either the narrow or the wide pattern.

3. Make a 2½″ slit in the middle of a short edge of your paper, corresponding to the line marked "cut" on the pattern. The two flaps of paper that result become the propellers. Fold one forward and one back.

4. Cut two slits below the propeller folds, as indicated on the pattern. Fold the vertical edges (marked "fold" on the pattern) toward the center. This will be the stem of the helicopter.

5. Fold the stem up at the bottom fold line, about half an inch from the bottom, as indicated on the pattern. This is the base of the helicopter. Add a small paper clip for weight.

6. Throw the helicopter into the air and watch it as it falls to the ground.

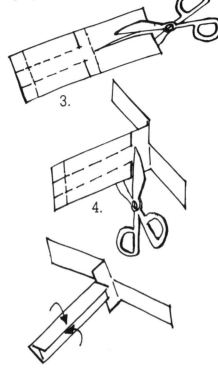

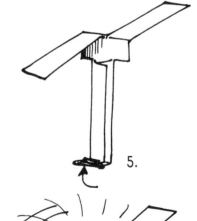

Name _____

HELICOPTER
Patterns

Make copies of this page to use with page 67.

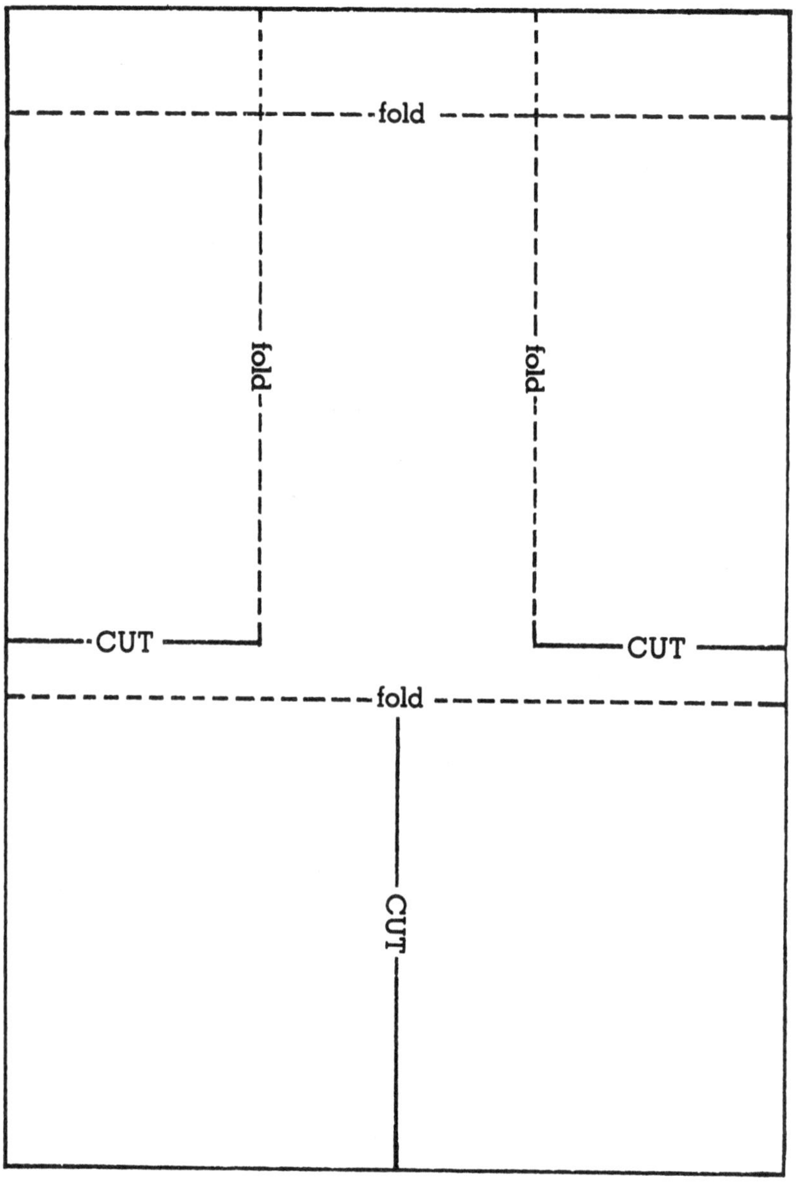

CUT

fold

CUT   CUT

fold   fold   fold

fold   fold   fold

CUT   CUT

fold

CUT

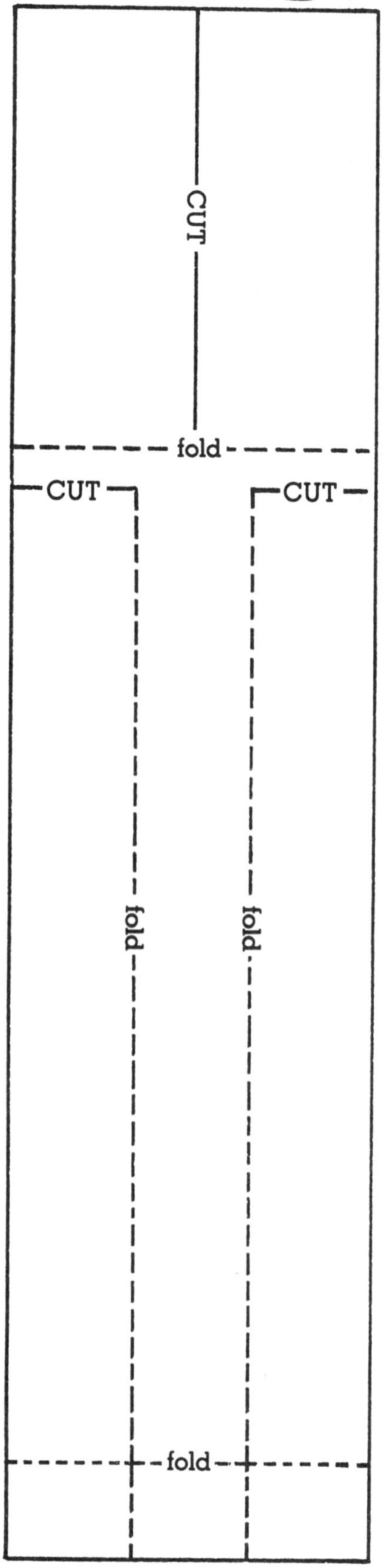

fold

CUT   CUT

THE
GAME MASTER
AWARD

for successfully completing
all projects and games

Presented to

_____
Name

By _____
Teacher

Date _____

Name _____

NUTTY MAZE

The big peanut below is a "nutty" maze! See if you can find your way through it. Start at the top, and trace a path from one box to another, using the key below. Each symbol in the key lets you move in a different direction, until you reach the bottom of the peanut.

70

Name _____

FEARFUL FLIBBERTIGIBBETS

The fearful Flibbertigibbets are a frightened bunch. They're afraid to talk to anyone, to work with anyone, even to walk down the same street with anyone! The only creatures the Flibbertigibbets don't fear are their own brothers and sisters. Look at the eight Flibbertigibbets below. They are standing on the pathways of the town park, too scared to move. Help them find the way to their brothers and sisters—without bumping into anyone else.

Use a pencil to trace the paths that will connect each brother-sister pair of Flibbertigibbets. But remember: Each one must not run into the wrong person <u>and</u> must not cross anyone else's path. Connect the following pairs:

A. Alfred Afraid to Alice Afraid
B. Freddy Fearful to Felicia Fearful
C. Sammy Scared to Sarah Scared
D. Tommy Timid to Teresa Timid

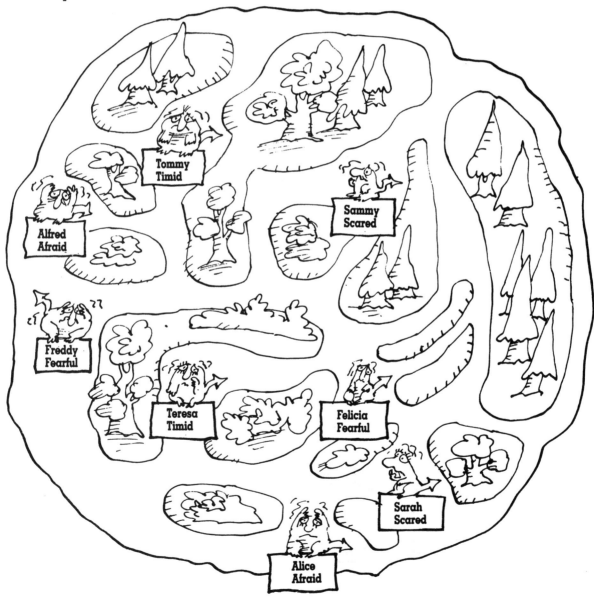

71

Name _____

TRACE-A-PATH

Have you ever noticed that people don't always understand each other's directions? Try this game and see if you can give and follow directions well. You will need a partner to play.

Materials: blindfold
two different-colored pencils
paper

Procedure:

1. Your partner puts on the blindfold. With one of the pencils, you draw a path on a piece of paper. You may not lift the pencil off the paper until you're done. The path can go in any direction, it can cross itself, and it can be easy or complicated. Put an arrow at the beginning of your path, and an **X** at the end.

2. Give the blindfolded player a different-colored pencil, and place the pencil point at your starting arrow. Tell that player you want him or her to trace over your path, following your directions. You can give any directions you want, but you may not touch the pencil or the other player's hand.

It's important to play the game at least twice so you can each try both parts. After each game, think about these questions, and discuss them with your partner:

1. How do the two paths (yours and your partner's) compare? Were they they same? If not, did they differ by much?

2. Did the other person understand your directions? Why or why not?

3. Were the other person's directions better or worse than yours? In what ways?

4. Could you give directions that the other person would understand better?

5. Could you think of a completely different way to successfully give directions?

Name _____

DOTS AND SQUARES

Here's a game you can play almost anywhere. You draw a number of dots on paper so that the lines connecting them will form squares of the same size.

Example:

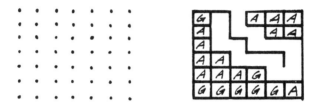

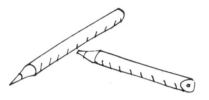

Materials: dot-boards on page 7 4
two pencils

Optional: 8½″ × 11″ lined or unlined paper

Procedure:

1. You may use the dot-boards on page 7 4 or create one of your own. Your dot-board may be a square or a rectangle.

2. One player begins by drawing a line connecting any two dots either vertically or horizontally. Then the other player does the same thing with two other dots. This continues until a square has been formed.

3. Players each have one turn until someone completes a square. As soon as a player's line completes a square, that player writes his or her initials inside it, and draws another line. If this other line completes another square, the player continues until he or she draws a line which does not complete a square. It is then the other player's turn.

4. If one player misses a chance to draw a line that completes a square, the other player may complete the square in his or her next turn.

5. The game ends when all the squares are filled in. Each player's squares are then counted, and the player with the most squares wins.

Look at the example above. Player A has filled in thirteen squares to player G's seven. But whoever plays next can fill in all the remaining squares on the board. Can you figure out how to do that?

Name _____

DOTS AND SQUARES

Name _____

SECRET CLUB

There is a secret club on the planet Gloonfark. Below are the rules for club membership. At the bottom of the page are 12 Gloonfarkians. Put an **X** on each Gloonfarkian who cannot join the club. Draw a circle around each Gloonfarkian who can join the club.

GLOONFARK SECRET CLUB RULES

1. All members must have two heads.

2. All member must have three eyes on one head and two eyes on the other head.

3. All members must have four arms.

4. All members must show teeth in both their mouths.

5. All members must have curly hair on at least one of their heads.

CRAZY QUADS

Mrs. Bird has a problem. She has identical quadruplets and can't tell them apart! She gave them all different hairstyles, but forgot which one wears which hairstyle. Help Mrs. Bird by following the directions below.

Read the directions carefully. On the chart, mark an **X** in the boxes of the hairstyles that each girl cannot have. Keep filling in **X**'s until there is only one blank box for each of the sisters. Put a ✔ in each of those boxes to show each girl's correct hairstyle.

1. Penny loves to pull on her sister's ponytail.

2. The sister with bangs plays with Penny, Annie, and Minnie.

3. Penny and Minnie are in the same class with the sister who has pigtails.

	PONYTAIL	BANGS	PIGTAILS	BRAIDS
PENNY				
JENNY				
ANNIE				
MINNIE				

Name _____

FLYING SAUCERS

Here comes an invasion of flying saucers! On each one is a message written in code. Follow the directions below to decode each message.

Write down the letter that the arrow indicates. Then, starting with the next letter, read clockwise around the flying saucer, counting by the number in the center of the saucer. For example, if the number is 2, read every other letter; if it is 3, read every third letter, and if it is 5, read every fifth letter. (A punctuation mark counts as a letter.)

A.

On the line below each flying saucer, write down the letters in the order that you find them by this method.

Keep going around the circle as many times as it takes to come back to the first letter. You will have gone around the circle the same number of times as the number in the middle of the saucer.

Group the letters into words and write the words on the second line under the saucer.

_____

_____

B.

_____

_____

C.

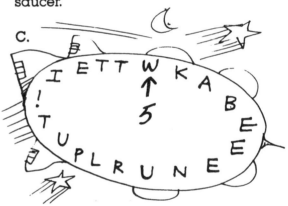

_____

_____

D.

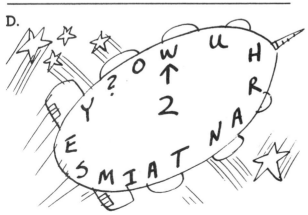

_____

_____

E.

_____

_____

Name _____

FRUITY TREE

Little Mary Sunshine has found a magic fruit tree! She can see that the tree grows several different kinds of fruit. But she can also see there are only a few ways to climb the tree and get all the fruits. Help Mary find the path to get all the fruits by following the directions below.

1. Look at the code key on the right. Decode the symbols, and write the letters on the fruits on the tree.

2. Trace the path through each symbol only once.

3. You will know if you have taken the right path if the decoded symbols spell out the names of all the fruits on the fruit crate below. You must pass through all of the symbols on the tree.

Code Key:

△ = a	⬭ = c	◇ = n
⬜ = e	▭ = g	△ = p
☆ = o	✚ = h	∂ = r
◯ = b	♡ = l	⬡ = y

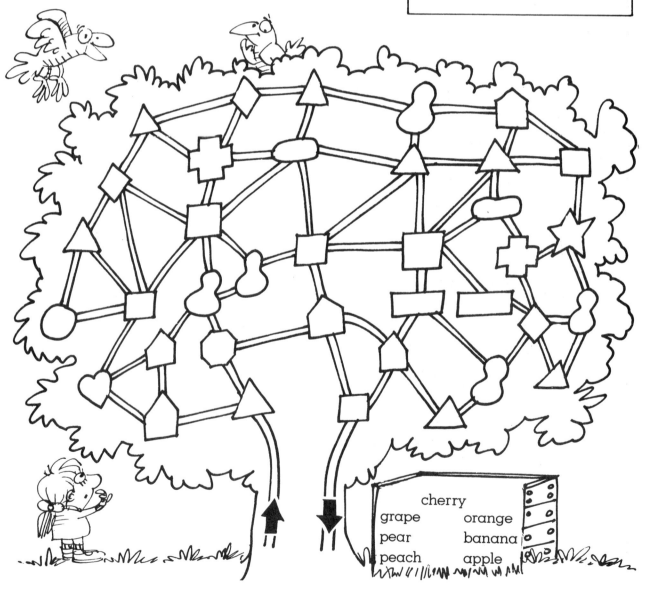

cherry
grape   orange
pear   banana
peach   apple

Name _____

ALL ROADS LEAD TO ROME

This is a very unusual maze because <u>all</u> roads lead to the city of Rome. However, only one route is the right one. To find it, follow the directions below.

Start where it says *ENTER HERE.*

1. Make a sharp left. Stop at the first tree.

2. Go three blocks north.

3. Go east past the last church.

4. Go south one block.

5. Go west six blocks.

6. Go north to the strange cave.

7. Go east to the fountain.

8. Go south one block.

9. Go west one block.

10. Go straight north to Rome.

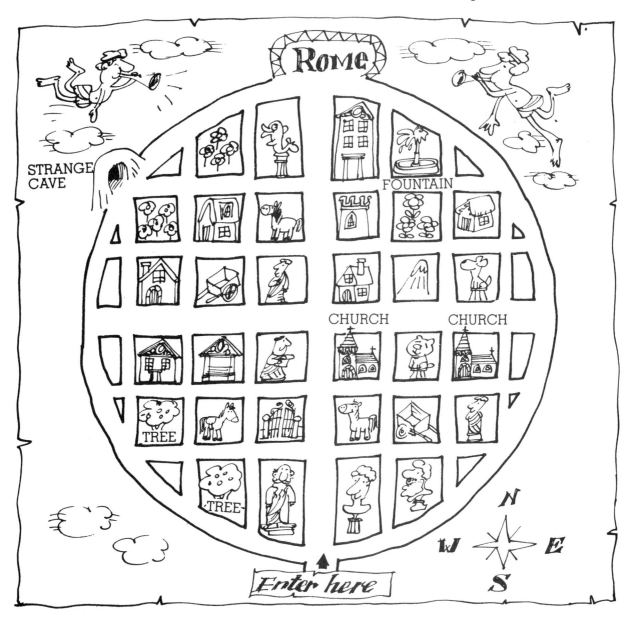

Name _____

TANGRAM TEASERS

A *tangram* is a Chinese puzzle made up of seven geometrical pieces. These seven pieces are called *tans.* You can fit the tans together to make many different shapes and designs. Here are some patterns you can make, using the seven tans:

You can make your own tangram by following the directions below.

Materials: pattern on page 81
               pencil
               ruler
               paste
               5″ × 6½″ square piece of
                  cardboard
               scissors
               crayons or markers

Steps:

1. Using a pencil and a ruler, follow steps 2-9 to connect the dots on page 81.

2. Connect point 1 to point 6.

3. Connect point 6 to point 5.

4. Connect point 1 to point 3.
Through which point do you have to go? _____

5. Connect point 3 to point 5.
Through which point do you have to go? _____

6. Connect point 1 to point 5.
Through which points do you have to go? _____

7. Connect point 2 to point 4.
Through which point do you have to go? _____

8. Connect point 6 to point 8.
Through which point do you have to go? _____

9. Connect point 2 to point 7.

10. Connect point 8 to point 9.

11. Paste the finished tangram on cardboard and carefully cut out the pieces. Color the pieces with crayons or markers.

12. See how many of the patterns above you can make using your seven tans.

13. Then, see how many different designs you can make by rearranging the seven tans. Try making a design, tracing an outline of it, and then challenging a friend to figure out how to make the pattern using your tans.

Name _____

TANGRAM DOT-TO-DOT

Follow the directions on page 80 to complete this page.

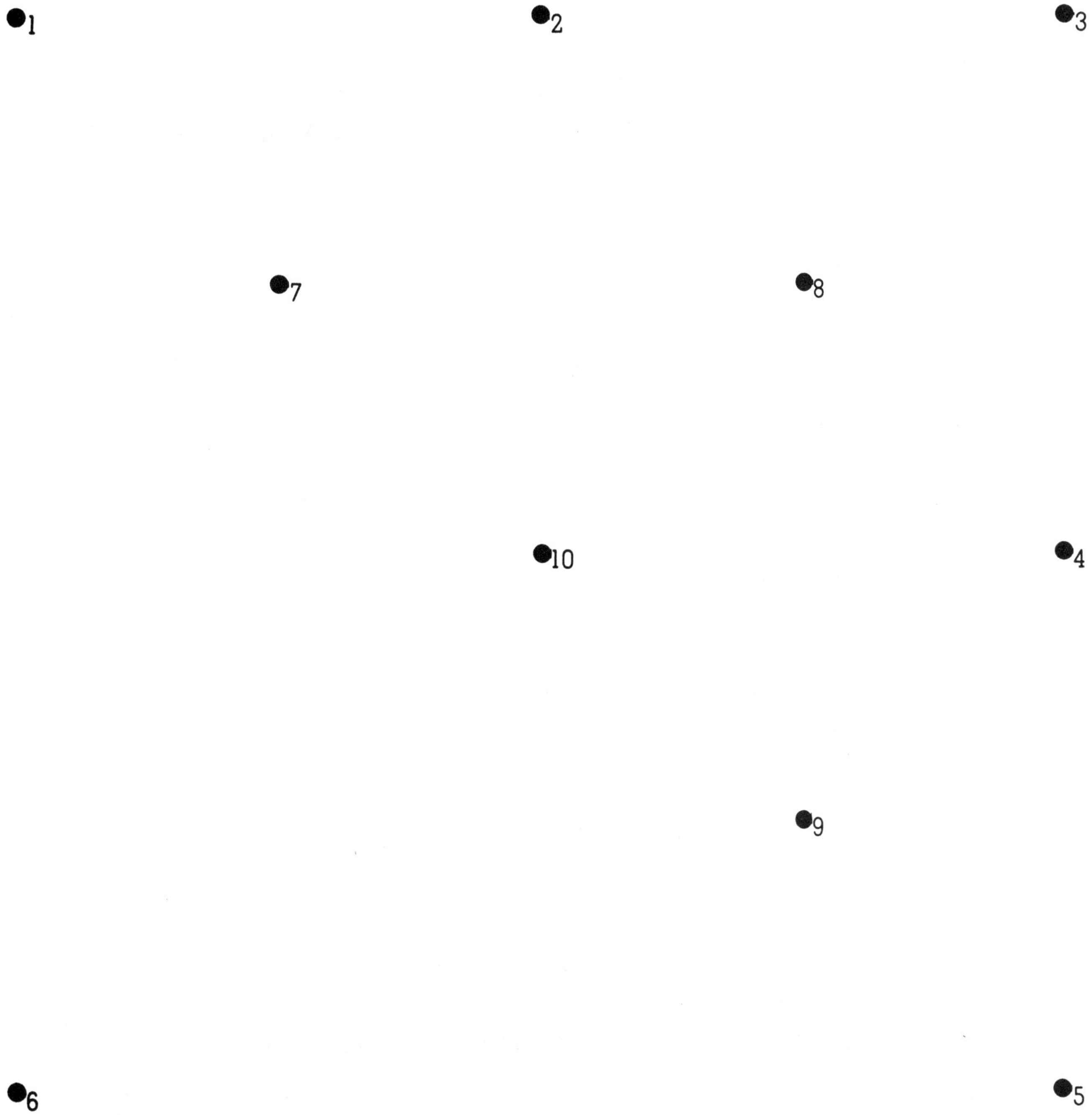

● 1
● 2
● 3

● 7
● 8

● 10
● 4

● 9

● 6
● 5

Name _____

CATEGORIES

Here is a fun game you can play almost anywhere. All you need is one or more friends and the materials listed below. Follow the directions to learn how to play.

Materials: two pieces of lined paper
two pencils

Procedure:

1. Each player draws a five-by-five grid, like the one at the bottom of the page.

2. Down the left side of the grid, write a five-letter word—one letter in each box, with no repeating letters. Examples are *snake, camel, dream, fight, loves,* and so on.

3. Across the top of the grid, write the names for five different categories, such as magazines, fruits, movie stars, TV shows, cartoon characters, books, songs, girls' names, games, animals, liquids, and so on.

4. Choose a time limit (10 to 20 minutes is usually enough, depending on how hard your letters and categories are), and fill in the *entire* chart, so that in each space you have an example (from the correct category) that begins with the correct letter of your word. In the example below, there is a magazine that begins with each letter, a TV show that begins with each letter, and so on.

	Countries	Girls' names	Flowers	Animals	Fruits and Vegetables
D	Denmark	Denise	Daisy	Deer	Date
R	Russia	Roseanne	Rose	Rabbit	Radish
E	Ethiopia	Ellen	Eglantine	Elk	Eggplant
A	Argentina	Anna	Anemone	Antelope	Apple
M	Mexico	Mary	Marigold	Moose	Mango

5. At the end of the time, everyone stops. In turn, players read their words out loud and total up their scores, according to the following system:

No score—if *everyone* has the same word in one space

  5 points—if one person has a word that no one else has

  10 points—if one person has a word in a space where no one else has any word at all

Because of this method of scoring, it's important not only to fill as many spaces as you can, but to try to think of words other people won't have.

Name _____

MRS. PERIWINKLE'S PUPPIES

Mrs. Periwinkle is taking her six prize-winning puppies to the local dog show. The dog show officials have given Mrs. Periwinkle directions about the order in which her dogs must walk. Read the directions carefully to help Mrs. Periwinkle figure out the order. On the lines provided below, fill in the correct order.

1. Palace Pal must walk directly in front of Prince Pitterpat and directly behind Prideful Prize.

2. Pom-pom-pom must walk directly behind Peachy Pooch and directly in front of Prideful Prize.

3. Perfect Pet must walk directly behind Prince Pitterpat.

4. Palace Pal must walk three places behind Peachy Pooch.

5. Read the directions again to help you complete the order in which Mrs. Periwinkle's prize-winning puppies must walk.

First _____

Second _____

Third _____

Fourth _____

Fifth _____

Sixth _____

Name _____

PUZZLING PLOTS

Farmer Franken has a large plot of land that he wants to divide among his five sons. The land is bordered by 16 logs of equal length. The land is to be divided among his five sons according to the following directions:

1. The sons must mark off their share of the land in order from oldest to youngest.

2. The sons must mark off their property with logs. The logs must be the same length as Farmer Franken's logs, and they must be placed as close together as the others are.

3. The eldest son and the second son must each use four additional logs to mark off property.

4. The eldest son may have as much property as he wants. All four younger sons end up with plots that are the same shape and size.

5. The third and fourth sons have only two extra logs each with which to mark off their property.

6. The fifth son gets the land left over.

How do the four youngest sons divide the remaining land among themselves?
Hint: Only the eldest son's plot is in the shape of a square.

JUST DESSERTS

Jackie is having a birthday party. Each of her six friends likes a different dessert. Jackie's having a hard time finding out which friends like which desserts, but she does have a few clues. Carefully read the clues below to help Jackie. On the chart below, put an **X** in each box beneath the desserts that each girl doesn't like. Remember, each girl will eat only one kind of dessert. Put a ✓ in the box that shows which dessert each girl likes.

1. Joan and Janet both hate caramel.
2. Janet, June, and Jenny are all allergic to bananas.
3. Once, when the class baked an apple pie, Jane and Janet wouldn't eat any of it.
4. Chocolate makes Jean, Joan, and June all break out.
5. Joan, Jenny, June, Janet, and Jane don't like oatmeal.
6. June, Jean, and Joan not only eat no ice cream but they never touch pie.
7. "Pudding is yucky!" say Jane and Jenny.
8. Jean and Jane say cake and candy make them sick.
9. Jenny says, "I don't like caramel because it gets stuck to my teeth."
10. Jenny and Janet like only chocolate and vanilla ice cream.

	Banana cake	Strawberry ice cream	Caramel candy	Oatmeal cookies	Apple pie	Chocolate pudding
Jean						
Joan						
June						
Janet						
Jane						
Jenny						

Answer Sheet for *Mind-Benders and Mazes*—Section 4

Fearful Flibbertigibbets—page 71

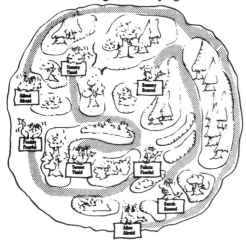

Secret Club—page 75

Gloonfarkians   7 and 9
can join the club.

Crazy Quads—page 76

	PONYTAIL	BANGS	PIGTAILS	BRAIDS
PENNY	✗	✗	✗	✓
JENNY	✗	✓	✗	✗
ANNIE	✗	✗	✓	✗
MINNIE	✓	✗	✗	✗

Flying Saucers—page 77

a. BEWARE OF FLYING SAUCERS.
b. GREETINGS, EARTH CREATURES.
c. WE LIKE PEANUT BUTTER!
d. WHAT IS YOUR NAME?
e. WHAT IS NEW, EARTHLING?

Fruity Tree—page 78

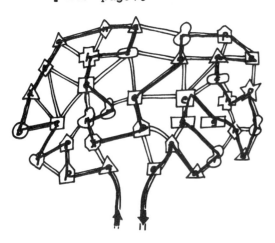

All Roads Lead to Rome—page 79

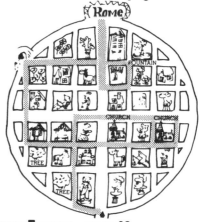

Tangram Teasers—page 80

4. 2   5. 4   6. 7, 10, 9   7. 8   8. 10

Tangram Dot-to-Dot—page 81

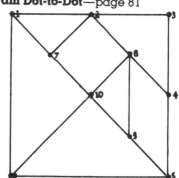

Mrs. Periwinkle's Puppies—page 83

First—Peachy Pooch; Second—Pom-pom-pom;
Third—Prideful Prize; Fourth—Palace Pal; Fifth—
Prince Pitterpat; Sixth—Perfect Pet

Puzzling Plots—page 84

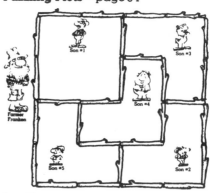

Just Desserts—page 85

	Banana cake	Strawberry ice cream	Caramel candy	Oatmeal cookies	Apple pie	Chocolate pudding
Jean	✗	✗	✗	✓	✗	✗
Joan	✓	✗	✗	✗	✗	✗
June	✗	✗	✓	✗	✗	✓
Janet	✗	✗	✗	✗	✓	✗
Jane	✗	✓	✗	✗	✗	✗
Jenny	✗	✗	✗	✗	✓	✗

Name _____

PADDLING ALONG

Read the passage below. When you come to a blank line in a sentence, read the words in the box. Choose the word that best fits in the sentence. Then write it on the line.

dance	humans
flyers	fast
fingers	swimmers
they	dogs
swim	arms

Thousands of years ago, humans probably learned to _____ to keep
from drowning. Most likely, _____ learned by watching animals swim.
The first human _____ probably used the "dog paddle" stroke. The dog
paddle was not the best stroke for _____ to use. Humans'
_____ and legs do not move the way animals' legs do.

Name _____

ANIMAL SILLIES

Look at each silly picture. Then choose the sentence that best fits what the **person** might say to the animal in each picture. Circle the letter of each correct sentence.

1.
   a. "Let's go to the playground."
   b. "I hope you're not hungry!"
   c. "I have a dog at home."

2.
   a. "I like to ride my bike."
   b. "Is this what you call <u>bearback</u> riding?"
   c. "Let's go to the store."

3.
   a. "What do you mean, 'meow'?"
   b. "I'd like to order some dog food."
   c. "Would you like to go to the **movies?**"

4.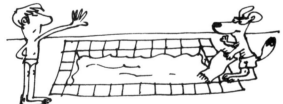
   a. "I'm sorry, sir. No dogs allowed."
   b. "How late is the pool open?"
   c. "Do I need a bathing cap?"

5.
   a. "I'd get there faster if I walked!"
   b. "You're too heavy."
   c. "My feet hurt."

Name _____

TOY STORE MATH

Diane and her family are at Tony's Toy Mart. They see many toys they like. Look at the price tags on the toys to figure out the answers to the questions below. In the column to the left of each question, darken the circle that has the letter of the correct answer.

ⓐ ⓑ ⓒ ⓓ 1. Diane has $6.00. What can she afford to buy?
   a. only the teddy bear   c. only the doll outfit
   b. only the baby doll   d. the teddy bear or the baby doll

ⓐ ⓑ ⓒ ⓓ 2. Mary Ann wants to buy the fashion doll and another outfit. How much money will she need altogether?
   a. $10.95   c. $17.90
   b. $16.95   d. $18.90

ⓐ ⓑ ⓒ ⓓ 3. Joe wants to buy the model airplane, but he has only $3.36. How much more money does he need to buy the airplane?
   a. $2.42   c. $9.06
   b. $12.42   d. $3.36

ⓐ ⓑ ⓒ ⓓ 4. Diane's mother bought the teddy bear, the board game, and the baby doll for Diane's birthday. How much money did her mother spend altogether?
   a. $8.99   c. $9.49
   b. $18.48   d. $12.98

ⓐ ⓑ ⓒ ⓓ 5. Sue has exactly enough money for the baby doll. How much more money would she need if she wanted to buy the teddy bear instead?
   a. $1.50   c. $5.50
   b. $ .51   d. $1.51

Name _____

MATCH THEM UP

Some tests you take have *matching questions* on them. A matching question will give you two lists of information and ask you to connect them in some way.

Be sure to read the directions carefully when you do a matching question. Then, use a *process of elimination* to match the items on the two lists:

1. First, match up the pairs that you *know* go together. When you've matched an item, cross out the number, so you know that you've already used it.

2. Then, with the remaining problems, if you're not sure which items go together, try to guess.

On the left of the chart below is a list of five math problems, numbered 1 through 5. On the right is a list of the solutions to these problems. On the lines provided, write the correct solution to each of the problems.

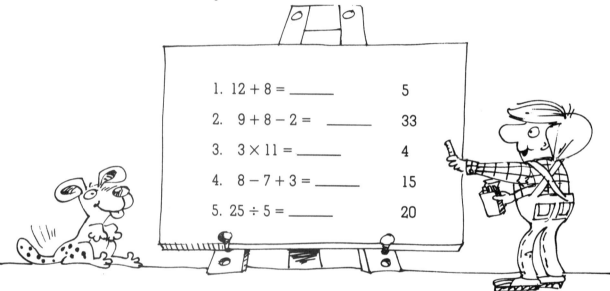

1. $12 + 8 =$ _____   5

2. $9 + 8 - 2 =$ _____   33

3. $3 \times 11 =$ _____   4

4. $8 - 7 + 3 =$ _____   15

5. $25 \div 5 =$ _____   20

Below are two lists of words. Each numbered word in the left-hand list rhymes with one word in the right-hand list. Sound out the words to figure out which ones rhyme. Then draw a line to connect the rhyming words.

6. skunk   sand

7. hand   mouse

8. bump   clock

9. house   stump

10. dock   trunk

CLASS QUESTIONNAIRE

Reproduce the questionnaire on page 92 and distribute to the entire class. The information gathered from these questionnaires can be used for a number of classroom or group projects. For example, a group of children could compile the information into any of the following displays:

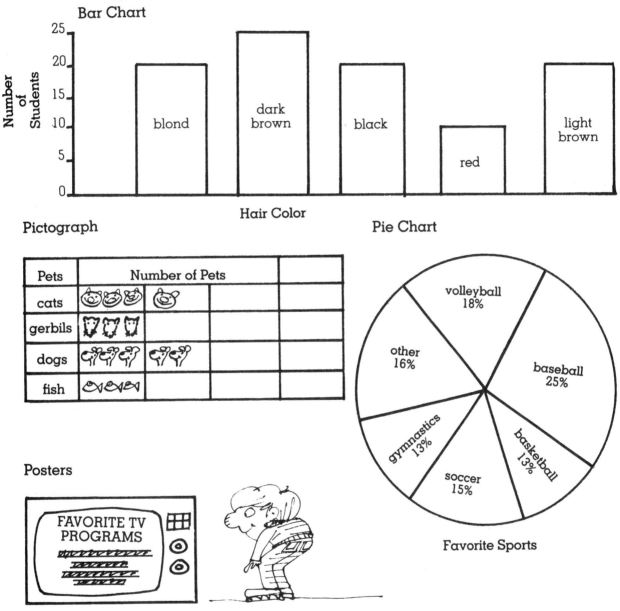

Bar Chart

Pictograph

Pie Chart

Posters

These displays could serve as a basis for discussions about polling, averages, and statistics. Advertising techniques that use such phrases as "four out of five people prefer . . ." can be discussed. Furthermore, the point can be made that information compiled from questionnaires is usually used to tell you about a group, but not an individual. For example, the class may earn an average of $5.00 per week, but that does not mean that every individual child earns that much.

CLASS QUESTIONNAIRE

The form below is called a *questionnaire*. It asks for information about you. Fill in all
the information requested.

Name _____   Date _____
     last   first   middle

Address _____   Class _____

_____   Number of students

Phone   (   ) _____   in your class _____

          area code   number   Name of teacher

Birthday ____ ____ ____   _____
        month   day   year

Height _____ Hair color _____   Name of school

Mother's name _____   _____

Father's name _____   _____

Do you have any brothers or sisters? ____ ____   If yes, how many of each? _____
                             yes no

_____

Do you have any pets? ____ ____   If yes, what kind? _____
               yes no

Favorite sport _____   Hours spent per week on sports _____

Favorite school subject _____   Hours spent per week on homework ____

Favorite TV program _____   Hours spent per week watching TV ____

Do you have extracurricular activities? ____ ____
                             yes no

If yes, what are they? _____

Do you have a job after school or on weekends? ____ ____
                                     yes no

If yes, what do you do? _____

Name _____

SUMMER CAMP

Everyone who wants to go to Camp Junebug has to fill out the application below.
Complete the application by following the directions and answering the questions on it.

CAMP JUNEBUG
36 Insect Lane
Buggywump, MD 92929

Please print clearly.

Camper's name _____ Age _____

Address _____ Birthdate _____

_____ Sex: M F

Parent or
guardian _____

Telephone number _____ Business phone _____

Name of school _____ Present grade _____

Favorite subjects _____

Hobbies or interests _____

_____

Can you swim? _____ Circle your preferences: canoeing hiking swimming
horseback riding   team sports   arts & crafts   archery

Have you been to camp before? _____ Which one? _____

Health Information

Do you have any allergies? _____ What kind? _____

Do you take any medication? _____ What kind? _____

Do you wear glasses? _____

Give name and telephone number of someone to contact in case of an emergency.

_____

Second graders attend Camp Junebug the first two weeks in June, third graders attend
the last two weeks in June, fourth graders attend the first two weeks in July, and fifth
graders have a choice of either or both of the remaining sessions.

Circle the session or sessions you are attending: June 1-15, 16-30
July 1-15, 16-31
Aug. 1-15

Name _____

BUBBLE BOOM!

Bertha Bubble wants to earn some extra money, so she is selling packages of Bubble Boom bubble gum. Below is a list of Bertha's first five customers. Under that is the order form she must fill in. Using the information in the list, help Bertha fill in the blank spaces in the order form. After you've completed the form, answer the questions on page 95.

Customer 1: Jane Blow, 334-9124, two packs of watermelon, two packs of grape, and one pack of original flavor

Customer 2: Joe Shmoe, 523-4968, one pack of each kind

Customer 3: Heidi Hoe, 883-9127, 10 packs of original Bubble Boom

Customer 4: Mary Joe, 456-6126, allergic to strawberry and grape; wants two packs of every other kind

Customer 5: Johnny Doe, 837-7513, three packs each of strawberry and cherry; one pack of all the others

BUBBLE BOOM ORDER FORM

Each package of Bubble Boom costs 35¢. Each package contains five slices of sugarless gum.

Date you must deliver Bubble Boom to customer: <u>May 1</u>. Please collect money on this date.

Please print.

Customer's name	Phone number	Straw-berry	Grape	Cherry	Water-melon	Orig-inal	Total packs	Total cost
						Order total		

Call in your Bubble Boom orders by April 15. Pick up on April 29.

Note to salesperson: You earn 10¢ for each pack of Bubble Boom you sell.

Name _____

BUBBLE BOOM!

Use the form and the information on page 94 to answer the questions below.

1. Which customer has ordered the largest amount of gum? _____

2. Which two customers ordered the same amount? _____

   and _____

3. How much does each pack of Bubble Boom cost? _____

4. How much does Bertha *earn* on this order altogether? _____

5. Which flavor of Bubble Boom did Bertha sell the most? _____

6. How many packs of Bubble Boom would you have to sell to *earn* $7.00? _____

7. What is the last date you can place your order? _____

8. When must you pick up the gum you ordered? _____

9. What day will you deliver the gum? _____

10. When do people pay for their gum? _____

Name _____

SPACE HELMET

Congratulations! The new space helmet you bought for your next intergalactic journey has just arrived. But you notice there's something else in the box along with your new helmet—a *warranty* card. Your warranty promises that the helmet you just bought is in working condition. If it is not, the Glommax Space Supplies Company will repair or replace it for free.

Look at the picture and information below. Follow the directions on the warranty card and fill in the necessary information.

GLOMMAX SPACE HELMET WARRANTY

Name _____   Age_____ Sex: M F

Address _____   Phone
                                    Number (___) _____

_____

Where   When
Bought _____   Bought _____

Name of   Model   Serial
Product _____ Number _____ Number _____

Please complete and mail this warranty card immediately. If anything goes wrong with the helmet within the next 12 months, Glommax will repair or replace it free. Be sure to keep a copy of this information and your sales slip or other proof of original purchase date.

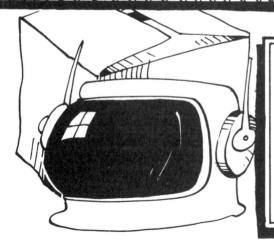

Product Information Form
Product Name: Glommax Space Helmet

Model no. 12/3456

Serial no. 1226651

Where bought: Glommax Space Supplies
1111 Story Street
Wilde, CA 92129

Date: 7/11/85

Name _____

MAKE A CHOICE

Some of the tests you take have *multiple-choice problems.* For multiple-choice problems, you must choose one correct answer from a group of possible answers. Read the sentence below. Look at the underlined word. On the right are four choices for the definition of that word. From the way the word is used in the sentence, see if you can choose the letter of the correct definition.

The gardener will <u>prune</u> the rosebushes.

a. a large goat
b. a dried fruit
c. cut off parts of a plant
d. show skill

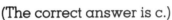
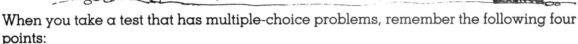

(The correct answer is c.)

When you take a test that has multiple-choice problems, remember the following four points:

1. Read the question or statement first. Try to answer it before you read the choices given.

2. Read all of the choices given before you choose one that you think is correct.

3. Choose the best answer. Several answers may be partly correct—so you must choose the best one.

4. If you don't know which of the answers is correct, eliminate the ones you know are wrong. From the ones that are left, choose the answer you think is best.

Read each sentence below. Then circle the letter of the best definition for each underlined word.

1. <u>Trace</u> the drawing.

a. lose
b. copy through thin paper
c. tear into small pieces
d. color the outlines of

2. Slow down and stop being so <u>impetuous</u>!

a. quarrelsome
b. lazy
c. noisy
d. hasty

3. Frank was <u>excluded</u> from the trip because he overslept.

a. eaten
b. pointed
c. floated
d. left out

4. I wanted to go to the new store after I received its <u>circular</u>.

a. leaflet that is given to many people
b. poster of some future event
c. round-shaped object
d. letter that demands payment

5. We were both <u>perplexed</u> by the mysterious noise.

a. puzzled
b. lost
c. tired
d. angry

Name _____

TRUE OR FALSE?

Some of the tests you take have *true/false questions.* True/false questions ask you to read a statement and judge whether it is true or false. For example:

In the sixth century B.C., the Greeks established mapmaking as a science. (Statement is true.)

Read the statements below. If any part of a statement is false, then the entire statement is false. On the lines next to each sentence, write *T* if the statement is true or *F* if it is false. You may use a dictionary or encyclopedia if you need help.

_____ 1. The robin is a bird that can fly.

_____ 2. The penguin is a bird that cannot fly.

_____ 3. The whale is a mammal that lives in water.

_____ 4. The dolphin is a mammal that lives on land.

_____ 5. The unicorn is a real prehistoric animal.

_____ 6. The dinosaur is a mythical prehistoric animal.

_____ 7. The platypus is a mammal that lays eggs.

_____ 8. The sea horse is a mammal that lays eggs.

_____ 9. The crocodile and the alligator are fish.

_____ 10. The orangutan and the chimpanzee are reptiles.

Name _____

AS MR. CROWE FLIES

Mr. Crowe is an English businessman. He has a very busy schedule. He has to fly from his home in London to three other major European capitals. But he doesn't know in what order he should fly to each one. Look at the map on page 100. Then read the instructions and the questions below. Use a separate sheet of paper to show your work.

On the lines provided for numbers 1–6, fill in the number of air miles Mr. Crowe will travel if he takes each of the following routes:

1. from London to Paris to Madrid to Rome _____

2. from London to Rome to Paris to Madrid _____

3. from London to Madrid to Paris to Rome _____

4. from London to Rome to Madrid to Paris _____

5. from London to Paris to Rome to Madrid _____

6. from London to Madrid to Rome to Paris _____

7. Which is the shortest trip? _____

8. Which is the longest trip? _____

9. If Mr. Crowe includes the final part of his trip back to his home in London, which two trips are the shortest distance? _____

10. Including the final part of Mr. Crowe's trip back to London, which two trips are the longest? _____

Name _____

AS MR. CROWE FLIES

Sometimes you face problems that ask you to show your work. When you solve problems like this, remember the following four points:

1. Use a pencil. In math, you often have to erase.

2. Show <u>all</u> of your work. Your teacher usually gives partial credit even if the final answer is wrong. The more work that you show, the more points you can earn.

3. Organize your work neatly on your paper so your teacher can follow it easily.

4. If you do not have time to finish a problem, outline the steps you would follow to solve the problem. Your teacher may give you partial credit for showing your understanding of the problem.

The map below contains the number of air miles between the different cities. Use this map to help you answer the questions on page 99. Use a separate piece of paper to show your work.

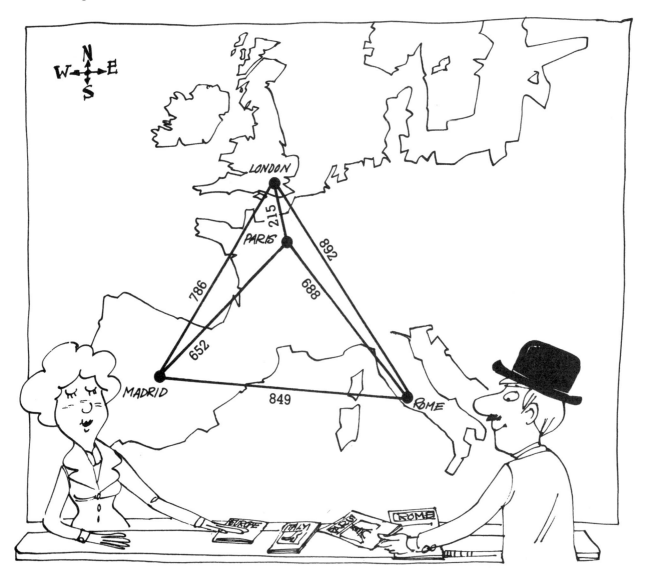

TEDDY'S BEAR

Read the story below very carefully. Then answer the questions about it on page 102.

America's favorite toy is named after President Theodore Roosevelt. Do you know what this toy is? It's the teddy bear.

In 1902, President Roosevelt was traveling in the South to settle a border dispute between Mississippi and Louisiana. He took some time off for a hunting trip in Mississippi. While he was on the hunting trip, he saw a bear cub in his rifle sights, but he refused to shoot it.

This event was reported in the newspapers. A newspaper cartoon about it was seen by Morris Michtom, a man who owned a small toy shop in Brooklyn, New York. Michtom made a brown plush bear with button eyes and put it in the window of his toy shop. He called the toy "Teddy's bear," and he wrote to the president, asking his permission to use his name. President Roosevelt wrote back, saying he didn't think his name would be useful in selling toys, but that Michtom was welcome to use it.

Michtom sold his first "Teddy's bear" in 1902 (later, they became known as teddy bears). It took a few years for them to become popular, but once they did, teddy bears sold more than any other toy. Other toy makers copied this idea. Within a few years, teddy bears were among the best-loved toys in America. Today the teddy bear is still America's favorite toy.

TEDDY'S BEAR

Read the story on page 101 carefully. Then read each question below and write in the answer if you know it. If you're not sure of the answer, look back at the story and try to find the information you need.

1. Who made the first teddy bear? _____

2. What did he do for a living? _____

3. What were the first teddy bear's eyes made of? _____

4. Where did the toy maker learn about the event that caused him to think of "Teddy's bear"? _____

5. For whom was "Teddy's Bear" named? _____

6. Why was this man traveling in the South? _____

   _____

7. What was he doing when he encountered the bear cub? _____

   _____

8. What did he think of the toy maker's idea? _____

   _____

9. In what year was the teddy bear first sold? _____

10. About how long did it take for the teddy bear to become popular? _____

   _____

Name _____

OUTER SPACE NEWS

Outer Space News is holding a contest. Read the contest advertisement below. Then follow the directions and fill in the entry form. After you have completed the form, answer the questions at the bottom of the page.

ENTER NOW!

Outer Space News

announces the
NAME-THAT-PICTURE CONTEST!

LAST DAY
TO ENTER
MAY 25

If your caption is chosen, you can win one of dozens of prizes!

1 **first prize**—a 35-mm camera plus $200 worth of film

2 **second prizes**—an instant camera plus $100 worth of film

5 **third prizes**—a pocket camera plus $50 worth of film

10 **fourth prizes**—an Outer Space News T-shirt

50 **fifth prizes**—a six-month subscription to Outer Space News

Plus: Everyone who enters will receive an Outer Space News button!!!!

Fill in the entry form below with your caption for this way-out photo!

Name _____   Age _____ Grade _____ Sex: M F
            (please print)   (circle one)

Address _____   City _____ State _____ Zip _____
            (street/apartment)

Phone: (_____)_____
            area code

Mail your entry to
Outer Space News
P.O. Box 2001
Neptune, NY 11357   Caption _____

Winners will be notified by mail about six weeks after the contest is closed.

1. What is the last date you can enter this contest? _____

2. How many prizes are there altogether? _____

3. When are the winners notified? _____

4. What does everyone receive for entering? _____

5. What is the fourth prize? _____

The Greatest
TEST TAKER
OF ALL

This is to certify that

_____
Name

has mastered with excellence
the test-taking technique

_____
Teacher

_____
Date

This is to certify that

_____
Name

_____
Address

_____   ☐   ☐
Age   M   F

is receiving this

FORMAL AWARD

for superior ability in
successfully completing
any and all types of forms

AWARD

_____
Teacher

_____
Date

Answer Sheet for *Tests and Forms*—Section 5

Paddling Along—page 87

1. swim
2. they
3. swimmers
4. humans
5. arms

Animal Sillies—page 88

1. b
2. b
3. a
4. a
5. a

Toy Store Math—page 89

1. d
2. c
3. c
4. b
5. d

Match Them Up—page 90

1. 20
2. 15
3. 33
4. 4
5. 5
6. skunk — sand
7. hand — mouse
8. bump — clock
9. house — stump
10. dock — trunk

True or False?—page 98

1. T   6. F
2. T   7. T
3. T   8. F
4. F   9. F
5. F   10. F

As Mr. Crowe Flies—page 99

1. 1,716   6. 2,323
2. 2,232   7. first
3. 2,126   8. fourth
4. 2,393   9. fifth and sixth
5. 1,752   10. second and third

Bubble Boom!—page 94

Customer's name	Phone number	Strawberry	Grape	Cherry	Watermelon	Original	Total packs	Total cost
1. Jane Blow	334-9124		2		2	1	5	$1.75
2. Joe Shmoe	523-4968	1	1	1	1	1	5	$1.75
3. Heidi Hoe	883-9127					10	10	$3.50
4. Mary Joe	456-6126			2	2	2	6	$2.10
5. Johnny Doe	837-7513	3	1	3	1	1	9	$3.15
						Order total	35	$12.25

Bubble Boom!—page 95 (cont.)

1. Heidi Hoe
2. Jane Blow and Joe Shmoe
3. 35¢
4. $3.50
5. original
6. 70
7. April 15
8. April 29
9. May 1
10. May 1

Teddy's Bear—page 102

1. Morris Michtom
2. He owned a small toy shop in Brooklyn, New York.
3. buttons
4. He saw a newspaper cartoon about Roosevelt and the bear cub.
5. President Theodore Roosevelt
6. He was settling a border dispute between Mississippi and Louisiana.
7. He was on a hunting trip.
8. He didn't think his name would be useful in selling toys.
9. 1902
10. a few years

Make a Choice—page 97

1. b
2. d
3. d
4. a
5. a

Outer Space News—page 103

1. May 25
2. 68
3. six weeks after May 25
4. an Outer Space News button
5. an Outer Space News T-shirt